"The One Page Business Plan
does something outrageous!
It causes very busy people
to stop and think.
As they start to write...
it confirms both their clarity
and their confusion!"

— Jim Horan
President
The One Page Business Plan Company

WARNING – DISCLAIMER

This book was designed to provide information in regard to the subject matter covered. It is not the purpose of this manual to reprint all of the information available to the author/publisher, but to complement, amplify and supplement other sources.

Use of The One Page Business Plan® does not in any way guarantee the success of an idea or organization, nor does it ensure that financing will be made available. When legal or expert assistance is required, the services of a competent professional should be sought.

The author/publisher shall have neither liability nor responsibility to any person or entity with respect to any loss or damage caused, or alleged to be caused, directly or indirectly by the information contained in this book.

If you do not wish to be bound by the above, you may return this book to the publisher for a full refund.

Published by:

The One Page Business Plan Company
1798 Fifth Street
Berkeley, CA 94710
Phone: (510) 705-8400
Fax: (510) 705-8403
www.onepagebusinessplan.com

ISBN-13: 978-189131501-5
ISBN-10: 1-891315-01-3

FIRST EDITION - v.1.1

Book Design: Melodie Lane
Cover Design: Jennifer Sbranti
Photography: Bryan Davis & Dirk Wentling
Print Consultant: Jim McCraigh
Media & Public Relations: Brad Kofoed

Printed in the United States of America

The One Page Business Plan®

for Women in Business

*The Fastest, Easiest Way
to Write a Business Plan!*

By Jim Horan & Tamara Monosoff

What Successful Women are Saying...

From $1 to $10 million in less than 5 years... with One Page Business Plans!

Practical, fun, and inspiring! Meeting Jim Horan and doing The One Page Business Plan at a SBA workshop in 2000 was absolutely invaluable to me as an entrepreneur and business owner. The return on investment of that $35 was incredible!

I used the One Page principles consistently while building my business, an organic beauty company that went from $1M to $10M in less than 5 years. Every year, my partner and each of my managers created One Page Plans for the New Year. They kept us focused, energized, motivated. I am certain the discipline required by writing and implementing our One Page Business Plans helped keep us on track to build the business I always dreamed of!

Building a business is hard work! One Page Business Plans will focus your efforts! This is the planning tool for anyone serious about building a business!

Christin Powell
Founder & CEO, Juice Beauty 2000-2007

The One Page Business Plan is a very versatile tool for all business brains. If you are a top level visionary, the One Page Business plan will help you fill in the details. If you are a detailed oriented planner, the One Page Business will help you see the "big picture".

Gail DaMert
CEO, DaMert Company 1990-2002

Most of us do reasonably well running our business by the seat of our pants, but if I would have had a One Page Plan when I started my business there is no telling where I would be now. Very Simple! Pragmatic! I recommend all women entrepreneurs utilize the OPBP as a key growth tool.

Deborah Johnson
President, RN, Certified Brain Injury Specialist, Careforward Inc.

I recommend The One Page Business Plan® to anyone wanting to free themselves from the fear and terror of writing a business plan. Jim's book is totally user-friendly, highly efficient, and best of all fun.

Jan St. John
Founder of 21st Century Radio Productions

I started using the One Page Business Plan 15 years ago at UC Davis. It was an incredible success in our University Fundraising and Donor Relations department of 96 employees. It worked beautifully in keeping a large group aligned and meeting our goals. Since then I have recommended it to everyone who wants to get clear on their goals and achieve them!

Luanne Stevenson,
President, Pajaro Group, Inc.

The One Page Business Plan provides students with what they will need as managers; a relevant, action oriented process. By working through the vision, mission, strategies, objectives and plans, they test the feasibility of their ideas and begin to understand the type and breadth of resources they need to build a viable business. First, they are appropriately overwhelmed by the challenges, but then recognize that they have also defined the steps to meet them. Once this process occurs, we have effectively conveyed the experience of management.

Elisabeth Watson
Adjunct Entrepreneurship & Finance Professor, San Francisco State

About One Page Business Plans

We have over 200 sales people from Group VPs to front line managers with One Page Business Plans. This process caused executives and peers to inspire and challenge one another and to collaboratively craft the best possible plans. What emerged were clear, well understood and, most importantly, aligned plans and commitments. This is a powerful process I highly recommend!

Nuge Ajouz
VP Sales Consultants, Oracle Corporation

The One Page Plan helped our management team obtain the results we need to succeed in this tenuous business environment. Starting with a clearly defined vision, supported by specific objectives, to the creation of strategies and action plans to make it happen, the Plan provides a clear path to focus our efforts off the trivial many to the vital few. The various graphs available (I love the visuals!) are an added advantage to track our progress and hold us accountable along the way!

Gwen Gallagher
President, Old Republic Home Protection

The One Page Business Plan is an exceedingly valuable tool for any organization, but I found it particularly helpful during the formation of my non-profit agency. Because non-profits typically deal with very tight budgets, even small mistakes can spell disaster. I used my One Page Plan to carefully and thoughtfully launch the non-profit and to date, my plan has proven its worth multiple times over.

Tracy O Tamura
Executive Director, Kidsteem™

The One Page Business Plan helped our sales team and the entire manager team stay strategic and on track even through the days of fire-fighting. I highly recommend The One Page Business Plan.

PJ Anderson
CEO, OP Contract
San Francisco Herman Miller franchisee

It's wonderful that someone finally came up with a business plan for independent professionals. It de-mystifies business planning so that the average business professional can actually write a business plan that makes sense!

Rebecca Salome Shaw
Entrepreneurial Authors

As the first woman superintendent of my district, I had to prove myself in many ways. Since placing OPBP in the hands of all leaders and teachers in the district, we have made great strides toward our goals. The school board, parents, community, and staff all are proud of the progress we are making. I attribute our focus and forward movement to our use of the One Page Business Plan. I strongly recommend the use of the One Page Business Plan to all women in leadership roles.

Sue Holmes
Superintendent, Cripple Creek-Victor School District

My first year as a rookie financial advisor was tough, I made only $13,000. Last year I made $250,000 and I mostly attribute it to having a OPBP for the last three years. After creating my plan, particularly my Mission Statement I stopped cold calling and started focusing on my LGBT community which was the reason I came into this industry. I love my One Page Plan!

Cheryl Rebottaro
Financial Advisor, Morgan Stanley

One of the biggest lies in business is that business plans have to be dozens of pages long to be impressive. I've built three businesses with the "One Page Business Plan". I was able to get funding, rent space to run the business, purchase inventory and develop ongoing strategies to grow my business by following my "One Page Business Plan".

Jessica Siegel
President, Harps Etc.

Foreword

Jim Horan

Planning is a dialog. It starts deep within you.

When it's appropriate... you will begin the process of exposing the dialog to your external world. The initial form may be written notes or informal discussions with people you trust. At the appropriate point, you will expand the dialog to your community. The dialog will grow stronger... or die. I've learned the keys to success are in us and our community... we just need to ask for the dialog, pay attention to what we hear, make our decisions, act on them... and then take the dialog to the next level.

A business plan is a collection of your intentions and decisions. Your Vision and Mission are vibrant, clear statements of your intentions. Strategies, Action Plans and Objectives reflect your decisions. You learned a long time ago about the importance of being clear on your intentions and making good decisions. The business plan is the place to do this work for your business.

I also believe your plan is a story, your story. I have come to believe the most important role for all entrepreneurs, business owners and executives is that of Chief Storyteller. When we share our story of what we are building, why we are building it, who we will serve and our plans for building our business...we are telling our story. When your story is compelling, people will listen and remember...and they will tell it to others. When enough people have heard your story, your business will move forward in all the ways you hoped it will, and also in ways you could never have imagined.

This book is the sixth in The One Page Business Plan series. It contains the simple, straight forward methodology I created 15 years ago, but it reflects the newest tools, techniques and exercises to help you get that inner dialog out of your head onto paper... so that you can refine it to the point that it reflects your best thinking. When your plan reflects your best thinking, you make it easier for others to understand what you are building. When they understand... they can and will step forward and be truly helpful.

I am delighted, and feel privileged to be coauthoring this book with Tamara Monosoff, creator of Mom Invented products and is known by the media as "America's Favorite Business Mom." We met early in her entrepreneurial path; I helped her write her first One Page Business Plan... and then stood back and watched her create a national phenomenon. Tamara truly understands business, knows how to inspire, coach and give very practical advice to women in business at every level from entrepreneurs to Fortune 500 executives. All while raising a family with her amazing husband.

I decided to invest the time to create this book because some of the most important things I have learned about life and business have come from women.

"Your plan is your story.

Take time to craft it carefully."

From my perspective, women tend to approach business from a place of openness, curiosity, receptivity, generosity, intuition and community more so than most men.

Also, many of the first One Page Business Plans that were created were with women. Several of these women, like Tamara have gone on to build very successful businesses in their city, state or nationally. All of these women attribute their success at some level, to the breakthroughs, insights and aha's they experienced in the creation of their One Page Business Plan. These same women cheered me on to productize The One Page Business Plan... and turn it into an international business.

This book is designed for women in businesses of all ages and stages of life. The process works equally well for first time entrepreneurs, corporate executives, non-profits, government and even life planning. At certain places in the book we give examples and templates for startups/small businesses and for larger, more established businesses, because their needs are different.

I have a special place in my heart for those women for whom entrepreneurship is a necessity, not a choice. I have done a lot of work with brave women who are building businesses because they are not employable, and their business is the only way for them to support themselves and their families. They have written some of the most amazing plans that I have ever read, and built very successful businesses.

Nobody ever built a business by themselves... it has always taken a village (thank you, Hillary Clinton). I believe the ultimate goal is to live, work and play in a manner that is consistent with who you really are and what is important to you!

Every word on your One Page Business Plan counts... don't rush the process! Beware of excessive verbiage! Remember: this is a marathon, pace yourself!

Most likely you will out-grow all of your plans.

You will stop planning when you stop breathing.

Now... go build a fabulously successful business!

Jim Horan
Founder & President, The One Page Business Plan Company

Introduction

*Tamara
Monosoff*

At the time of publication of this book, it was just over six years ago that I met Jim Horan, Founder of the One Page Business Plan company.

For me to explain why I am such a believer in the power of the One Page Business Plan, I'll have to step back for a moment. One stop along my path was as an advisor in the White House during the Clinton Administration where I was serving on the President's Initiative on Race. I was working with another senior advisor in White House Communications and sharing some of my ideas. She said, "No matter how good your idea is, no one will read it, understand it, or implement it unless you can get it on to one page." It was gratifying to later see some of my ideas and programs mentioned by President Clinton and the Secretary of Education after I learned the impact I could have with one page.

This served me well later when I was preparing to present my doctoral dissertation proposal to the dissertation committee at the University of San Francisco. I had decided to present the entire doctoral proposal in one page. After briefly presenting my one page proposal, there was a deafening silence in the room during which I felt the blood drain from my head -- no one said a word. Then, after what felt like hours but was really only moments, the Chairman held up the one page proposal and said, "In thirty years, no one has presented their doctoral proposal in one page. I think this should be our new model." From these experiences, the power of one page had proven itself to me.

Fast-forward to early 2003 where I was a new mom of a two-year-old and a newborn, out of the workforce, and brimming with new ideas.

I had been speaking with my husband about my new invention idea. One day he told me about a business planning workshop being hosted by our local Chamber of Commerce. Up to that point, the notion of writing a "business plan" seemed like something done in an MBA program, which did not apply to "me." I attended the One Page Business Plan workshop led by Jim and immediately saw how wrong I was and that I could create a plan and build a real business.

Today my business is still a work in progress but I can say that a lot has transpired since that initial workshop. My products are sold in 9,000 stores throughout the United States, Europe and Australia. I have written three books, built a website www.mominventors.com and online community to inspire and impart information to support other women in business, and have spent the last six years working from home with my business partner (husband), and raising my two daughters.

> *"It became clear that women needed and deserved to have their own business planning book without business jargon or techno-talk!"*

Since that day, I have recommended Jim Horan's One Page Business Plan at every possible opportunity. However, over the past six years during countless conversations with women in business, it has become clear to me that women often avoid and resist the planning process. Explanations I often hear are, "I don't know how to start a plan," "I don't understand the numbers," "I'm afraid I won't get it," I'm too busy," or "I'm the idea person... I'm not good at planning and implementing." It became clear that women needed and deserved to have their own business planning book without business jargon or techno-talk – but instead authentic stories and examples from real women navigating their way and building a plethora of businesses on their own terms.

I am exceedingly grateful and excited that when I proposed this collaboration, Jim immediately embraced it.

Together we have created an approachable, business planning workbook for you. The One Page Business Plan for Women in Business combines Jim's proven methodology with the colorful stories, sample business plans, and voices from women just like you and me!

It took three times for me to really learn this "one page" lesson which is partly why I am so adamant about sharing it with you.

I hope you'll embrace this workbook and treat it like a friend. Don't be surprised. You may just fall in love with your business plan!

With heartfelt appreciation for each of you!

Tamara Monosoff
Founder & CEO, www.mominvented.com

VISION
MISSION
OBJECTIVES
STRATEGIES
ACTION PLANS

Table of Contents

The First One Page Business Plan
Was Written by a Woman

*Jessica
Siegel*

It had always been my dream to create a community music program in my city. I was fortunate to grow up in Philadelphia where I was able to study music at the Settlement Music School. The school provided music education and performance opportunities to all members of the community regardless of one's ability to pay, age, musical ability and previous experience. The Settlement Music School provided me with my music lessons and a firm foundation for my career in music.

In 1995, my performing career came to a screeching halt from an injury. I saw that this was my time to develop my vision of creating a local community school. It became quickly apparent that people thought I had a good idea, but they wanted to see a written business plan before committing their resources to the project. Having never even seen a business plan, I went to the bookstore to find help on the topic. I was quickly overwhelmed by the amount of literature on the topic. All of the books were thick tomes of information. I bought one that looked user friendly, but all that happened was I was paralyzed by all of the analysis and business jargon.

Around this time, I met Jim Horan in a business group. Jim introduced me to his book, "The One Page Business Plan". I was full of trepidation and feeling very discouraged. I was overwhelmed by information, ideas, words and processes that I didn't understand. Jim suggested that we meet for a bicycle ride in the nearby park and chat about my idea.

The next Saturday, Jim and I went for the most memorable bike ride of my life. We rode to the end of the bike path in the Berkeley hills and settled ourselves in the grass. We had a 360 degree view of the San Francisco Bay Area. The sun was shining, a light breeze cooling us. Blue skies were everywhere. The place is appropriately nicknamed Inspiration Point. In this spot on the planet, one could only feel that anything was possible. Even writing a business plan!

Jim then took out a small, battery operated tape recorder and asked me to start talking about my idea for the music school. I started to share my vision and ideas on how to find funding, teachers, equipment and a facility. Jim asked me questions along the way, coaxing me to flesh out thoughts and think of other challenges in my way of bringing life to my vision.

We talked for two hours. At the end, Jim turned off the tape recorder and announced that we now had a business plan! Everything was in my head. I just needed help organizing it. Jim had the tape transcribed. We met a few weeks later to transfer the plan onto his "One Page Business Plan". Jim explained that everything HAD to be on one page. This one rule helped me to clearly synthesize our long conversation into focused, succinct thoughts and actions. In an hour we had a complete business plan.

Over the next few weeks I shared the plan with major funders of the arts in our county and was able to receive seed money to begin the school. The Community School of Music was created, funded and had a home of its own. In 1996, the school started with a pilot program of 25 students and has grown to serve over 500 students of all ages, financial status, experience and ability throughout the Bay Area.

"The One Page Business Plan" and Jim's gentle coaching made this vision a reality. The "One Page Business Plan" is a stroke of genius. Anyone can use this plan! Over the years, I have returned to the book to refocus my business and grow two more music businesses. I even found that the structure and clarity of the Plan work well for marketing plans and general goal setting. I recommend the book to everyone. It doesn't matter if you've written dozens of lengthy, wordy traditional business plans or if this is your first one. The plan works. It's simple, fun to use and will help you bring your vision to a reality.

Crazy Single Mom Changes her Life

Cheryl Rebottaro

When I met Cheryl Rebottaro, she was a rookie financial advisor recently hired by Morgan Stanley. I was working with the rookie and under-performing advisors. After Cheryl returned from corporate training where she had been shown what to sell and how to sell it, I found her in her office cold calling out of the phone book. She was frustrated and as she says, "a crazy single mom trying to make it."

As Cheryl and I sat together, I asked her the questions that are the foundation of a One Page Business Plan and her story unfolded. Cheryl had been working nights for 20 years as a singing waitress and picking up extra cash singing in a band on the weekends. Deep down Cheryl knew that somehow she would change that. One of her band mates suggested she interview with his employer, Morgan Stanley. She prayed for change, bought a suit and with no college education, was hired immediately.

Fast forward 10 months to when I met Cheryl. I asked her why she was cold calling. She said her number of dials was measured and this was a way to stay employed even though 8 out of 10 dials were on the "do not call" list and the other 2 out of 10 were crazy, lonely or just bad clients. I asked her who did she want to be in service of? She said "women in transition and the LGBT community, both of which are horribly underserved." I asked her what she wanted to accomplish as a financial advisor; she said "I want to be a trusted advisor, not a sheister!" As she wrote her One Page Business Plan she now had target markets to go after and she knew exactly how to do that! These were the people she wanted to be with! Her plan simply flowed out of her then.

In that first year she made $13,000 and last year she made $250,000. She says the value of having a One Page Business Plan is "it helped me understand my real business model and simplify it enough for it to be achievable. Working one to one with someone who understands the process helped me prioritize and take steps month by month to achieve measurable results."

In a frame by her desk is Cheryl's Mission statement: *I Consciously Care About My Clients & Deliver Their Highest Good*. And she does.

Written by Toni Nell, Springboard Consulting
(Cheryl's One Page Business Plan Coach/Advisor)

The Story Behind
Clarine's Florentines

*Clarine
Hardesty*

Clarine Lim Hardesty grew up in Southern California, with most of her summers spent traveling to be with her grandparents in Jakarta, Indonesia. She learned early she loved traveling. During her college years she spent a summer in Florence, Italy and found food to be another passion in her life. After she ate her way through Europe, she obtained her Teaching Credential and Masters Degree in Education from the Dominican University of California. She then went on to teach the 2nd grade in San Francisco. Clarine and her husband, Colin, now live in Lafayette, California.

After years of commuting to San Francisco, Clarine decided to leave teaching to follow in her grandmother's footsteps as a self taught baker. Growing up, Clarine and her mother baked Florentines every year as holiday gifts for friends and family... and each year her father, being an entrepreneur himself, would say to her, "You should really start selling Clarine's Florentines."

Two years ago, she started renting space from a local bakery twice a month and enlisted her husband as free labor! Clarine's Florentines was born! Creating a business from the ground up allowed Clarine to be creative and make her own decisions but with no training or schooling in business, she was faced with learning accounting, marketing, purchasing and sales first-hand. Clarine's Florentines now leases its own kitchen in Berkeley, with two part-time employees and distributes Florentines to approximately twenty gourmet food stores in the SF Bay Area.

One of the most enjoyable aspects of her business is handing out samples. About six months after starting her company, Clarine had a conversation with a customer. He suggested The One Page Business Plan book and mentioned that because of its simplicity, anyone can write a business plan using this technique.

As she completed a draft of her OPBP her whole outlook about the success of her company changed. She felt so accomplished knowing that she had taken her first step in developing a vision, mission, objectives, strategies and action plans! A plan! It gave her piece of mind to have a clearer, more focused direction in which to take her company. It amazed her that she could describe complex strategies, objectives and action plans, so clearly and simply... on a single line. She knows the plan will continually evolve as the company does, but the rewards that she gained and the confidence she acquired by creating the OPBP were immeasurable.

Clarine's sage advice: Talk to others! Even though it may seem as an entrepreneur one is alone, there are so many people willing to help out. Some of the best advice, surprisingly, came from people she thought were competitors. They actually turned out to be cheerleaders!

Clarine's Florentines

Clarine Hardesty

President

vision

Within the next 5 years grow Clarine's Florentines into a $500,000 gourmet food manufacturing company that nationally distributes and sells the most delectable Florentines available to gourmet food enthusiasts, specialty & premium food markets, high-end restaurants and other gourmet food manufacturers. Also, within the next 5-10 years make Clarine's Florentines a profitable and appealing enough business to sell. Grow owner compensation to $100,000 per year by year 5.

mission

We hand make elegant cookies that people crave and never forget!

objectives

- Grow sales from $25,000 in 2009 to $60,000 in 2010.
- Achieve pre-tax profits of $5k in 2009; minimum of $30,000 in 2010.
- Maintain gross profit margin at 44% in 2009, grow to 46% in 2010.
- Increase holiday sales from $16,000 in 2009 to $25,000 or more in 2010.
- Increase # of in-store demos from 8 to 16 starting Feb 1st.
- Increase # of active stores from 16 to 45 by Dec 31st.
- Increase cases sold per month from 24 to 48 effective Jan 1st.
- Increase production yields from 88% to 96% for each batch.

strategies

- Promote hand-made, gluten-free, European inspired, gourmet qual. thru creative pkg/PR/web.
- Increase # of high-end gourmet stores through personal marketing & referrals.
- Promote initial trial w/ in-store demos, free restaurant trials & individual serving packaging.
- Use Internet to sell products w/ online store, promote demo locations & share stories/recipes.
- Attract media attention w/creative stories; participate in nat'l trade shows for brand visibility.
- Creatively partner w/ other small gourmet food companies; create news w/ the Sweet Mafia.
- Lease commercial kitchen & sublet to other mfg'ers to improve quality & reduce expenses.
- Enhance productivity and accountability of employees through training and modeling.
- Have fun! Stay balanced! Have plenty of time for my new family! Enjoy life!

action plans

- Complete lease negotiations, facility rehab & move in by Oct. 15th
- Introduce Re-Packaging and Individually Wrapped products by Oct. 31st.
- Hire part-time person for in-store demos by Feb 1st.
- Launch Monthly Newsletter by April 1st.
- Participate in first Trade Show by January 31st.
- Launch On-line Store & expanded website by March 30th.
- Launch Gourmet Store Target Market Campaign on June 1st.
- Take two week vacation in July; have 1st baby in 2nd half 2010.

The Story Behind
Galaxy Group

*Karen
Horrigan*

Karen Horrigan is the owner and President of Galaxy Group, a promotional products company. Galaxy Group was founded in 1978 and purchased by Karen's family in 1986. She watched her parents run the company for most of high school and college, and in 1992, Karen took over the family business.

Karen loves being a business owner. As a mom, she really values the flexibility it has offered her... something that she would not have with a traditional job. Over the years, she has been able to slow down when necessary (definitely when she had her two children), and pick up the pace when she was ready. Karen lives in Walnut Creek, CA with her husband Mathew and her two children, Graham (8) and Paige (5).

Business has been good for Galaxy Group over the years. But, Karen began to see that technology was making some major changes to the industry, and she knew she had to make some changes in her business to keep up. It was time to get focused and be extremely clear about the direction she wanted the company to go in. "Timing was perfect!" Karen said about her introduction to The One Page Business Plan. She was invited to a planning workshop for women business owners... and curious enough to attend. "It turned out to be exactly what I needed at exactly the right time!"

Even though the company has been in existence since 1978, Galaxy Group never had a business plan. Even after Karen finished her MBA program at UC Davis, she still felt overwhelmed by the idea of creating one. But, The One Page Business Plan took the fear out of this process... made it seem doable! "Not to say that the process was easy. In fact, I was surprised at how much it made me think... think about things that (in 18 years of business) I had never thought about before!"

Karen says her biggest struggle throughout the process was clearly defining her target/ideal customer. At the beginning of the process, she thought her target customer was "small to medium-sized businesses." We challenged her to put a face on her ideal customer... who did she really want to work with? As she dug deeper, she said that she wanted to work with companies that "value brand consistency." We challenged her again, and as she dug deeper, she said that not only should they value brand consistency, but they should "have an in-house marketing department and a budget for promotional products." Now that is quite clear!

Karen's advice to other women in business: "You can't be everything to everyone! Be very clear about what you do... and who you want to work with. After 18 years of owning this business... I FINALLY DO!"

Galaxy Group

Karen Horrigan
President

vision

Within the next 1.5 years grow Galaxy Group into a $1.3 million national promotional products company. We provide customized marketing products utilized in trade shows, sales incentive programs and customer/employee gifts. Our ideal client is a growing company with an in-house marketing department who values brand consistency.

mission

THE source for promotional products that make you say WOW!

objectives

- Increase annual sales from $728K in 2008 to $1.3 million in 2010.
- Grow pre-tax profits from $96K in 2008 to $180K in 2010.
- Add 25 new accounts for 2nd half of 2009; 100 in 2010 for a total of 375 accounts.
- Increase average sale from $1500 to $2500 by 2010.
- Win 95% of client proposals in 2010 from 80% in 2009.
- Increase repeat orders from current clients by 20% or $50K by 2010.
- Increase customer/prospect follow up from 15/day/salesperson to 20/day/salesperson.
- Attend 4 industry trade shows in 2010, from 1 in 2008; generating $25,000 in sales.

strategies

- Target companies with in-house marketing departments thru mailings/online marketing.
- Focus on customers who value product knowledge and professionally printed materials.
- Create new online customer opportunities by using Google AdWords/Constant Contact.
- Pricing strategy: to provide fair pricing and to match competitors when needed.
- Strengthen marketing by implementing quarterly promotions , both email and mail.
- Enhance implementation by setting definite deadlines.
- Improve customer reorders by sending reorder notices and discount coupons.
- Narrow online products to 5 vendor lines so that discounts can be negotiated.

action plans

- Research/compile list of local companies with promotional budgets of $20K by Jan 15th.
- Send reorder notices with coupon by Jan 31st.
- Work with designer to polish printed materials and website by April 30th.
- Activate Google AdWords advertising campaign and run test ads side by side by July 15th.
- Implement Constant Contact Quarterly Blasts by Sept 1st.
- Begin quarterly catalog/flyer mailings Oct 1st.
- Reward customer loyalty with high quality year end gift, Dec 15th.

The Story Behind Optimum Living

Tonya Dorsey

Optimum Living was founded in October 2005 and includes my coaching, consultation, speaking and writing endeavors. The company is based in the Washington D.C. area with clients country wide. Currently, I am providing personal and executive coaching, consultation and training as well as keynote addresses. I recently published my first book, *From Crisis to Purpose: A Mother's Memoir,* and am developing ideas for the next one.

At the time I launched Optimum Living, I was looking for a new outlet for my interest in growth and development to channel my interests in speaking, writing and working with people. For thirteen years, I had worked as an Associate Pastor of a church as the Director of Family Life. I was pursuing a counseling degree, planning to become a psychotherapist. After I started masters work in counseling, I wondered, "Once a person has worked out problems of the past through counseling, where do they go to design a future? What if a client has opportunities and needs help building a strategy? What about people who want to build on strengths and enhance leadership?"

I worked on a traditional business plan and the initial business development work of designing a website and stationary, setting up a blog, and seeking clients. My business expanded into both personal and professional development. I wrote and released my first book, *From Crisis to Purpose: A Mother's Memoir,* for people who are coping with unexpected loss. Opportunities increased and my initial business plan was soon outdated. There was so much going on at that point, I needed a way to focus and plan.

I met a fabulous coach, Pat Mathews of Breakthroughs for Your Business, who introduced me to The One Page Business Plan. Once again, I found EXACTLY what I was looking for.

I told her about the need to organize and manage my business endeavors. Pat asked the right questions and helped me develop a draft. In a matter of two or three coaching sessions, along with some brief follow up between sessions, I had my plan.

I could not believe how easy it was!

I was more than pleased with the result. It's one page, so I can post it for continued reference. The language is understandable. The format is straightforward, and it is easy to update year after year. For business owners who need to plan and want to avoid the complicated and overwhelming process of writing a traditional business plan, I would highly recommend the One Page Business Plan.

Optimum Living, LLC

Tonya Dorsey
Owner

vision

By year-end 2012 grow Optimum Living, LLC, into a $150,000 coaching and consultation company based in the Washington, D.C. area and internationally known for delivering high energy keynote addresses, authoring timely, thought provoking and personally supportive books and articles, and providing individual and group coaching to Generation X women who struggle with significant transitions and major life changing events.

mission

Help Generation X women uncover their possibilities and live life to the fullest.

objectives

- Increase total revenue from $25,000 to $100,000.
- Sell 2000 copies of new book in 2010. Q2 400, Q3 600, Q4 1000.
- Increase number of major speaking engagements from 6 to 15.
- Ship 100 % of book orders within 7 days of receiving request.
- Boost passive income from $0 to $10,000.
- Grow mailing list from 532 to 1,000.
- Increase avg monthly billable individual coaching hours from 10 to 20.

strategies

- Use Internet/Technlgy to promote biz, deliver prod/svcs, communicate/clients & keep records.
- Mkt biz w/quality written & electrnc promo matls, networking, pub spkg & media exposure.
- Establish follow-up consistency w/ good tracking & record keeping, routines & scripts.
- Focus biz w/OPBP, biz coach, de-cluttering office environ & dev efficient systems/processes.
- Incr profit w/new coaching clients, add'l spkg gigs, book publ(s) and incr billable hours.
- Generate passive income w/affiliate mktg, refl programs, writing/publshg & other prod dev.
- Assure nat'l exposure w/book tours, blog, website, keynote addresses & nat'l media attention.
- Grow mailing list w/website freebies/public spkg/class sign-ups/word of mouth/networking.
- Create fulfilling pers life w/space for pers grwth/hlthy living/fun/energetic family relships.

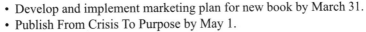

action plans

- Develop and implement marketing plan for new book by March 31.
- Publish From Crisis To Purpose by May 1.
- Complete One Page Business Plan by May 15.
- Implement systems and protocols plan by July 1.
- Intro at least 1 additional passive income stream by July 15.
- Complete new book proposal by Aug 1.
- Submit publishing package to selected publishing houses by Sept 1.
- Complete mailing list blitz by Oct 31.

The Story Behind
Educate Advocate Now

Greta
Olano

I am Greta Olano, a loving mother of two, an educator for over 14 years, and now a small business owner! I live in San Ramon, CA with my children, Olivia (2nd grade) and Luca (Kindergarten). Before beginning my career as an educational consultant and small business owner, I taught elementary school for many years. I have always loved working with children, but it was my own daughter, Olivia, who made me realize my true passion wasn't teaching. My passion was coaching and advocating for children with AD/HD and providing support to their families.

In 2005 I started working as a private tutor to make extra money. I began noticing that the majority of the children I worked with had some sort of learning or behavioral challenge; their parents didn't know where to turn, their teachers were frustrated. Then in 2007 my daughter Olivia was diagnosed with AD/HD and Sensory Integration Disorder. What's worse, Olivia's teachers were frustrated with her, and Olivia's self esteem was plummeting. Now it became my mission and passion to find a way to help Olivia and children like her. I started my business, Educate Advocate Now, in June 2009.

As my client base increased, my services expanded and I quickly progressed from private tutor to educational consultant, coach, and advocate. Juggling two children as a single mother, a full time job at school, and a rapidly growing educational consulting business quickly became overwhelming.

I am an educator and knew nothing about starting a business, and to be honest I didn't think I needed to know anything about business. I thought business plans were for people with lots of money, many employees, and corner offices with windows overlooking the San Francisco Bay. Then one day I ran into Tamara Monosoff and she offered me an opportunity to participate in a workshop for women on how to write a business plan. I had no idea she had just given me the opportunity of a lifetime! I remember chuckling to myself thinking how ridiculous it was for me to even ponder the idea of a business plan, but I had already taken a huge leap of faith so I figured if nothing else I'd get to meet some other women in business and network a bit.

Tamara sent me an email that same day introducing me to the One Page Business Plan. I have to admit it was a huge relief to see the words "ONE PAGE!" A few days later I was given instructions how to begin writing my plan and I found the instructions and the lessons to be very intuitive and helpful. I had the privilege of participating in a hands-on workshop with a group of women also new to the One Page Business Plan which was led by Tamara and Jim Horan. I couldn't believe I was actually learning about visions and missions and objectives and then it hit me... I had started a REAL business! I left the workshop that day with the most powerful tool for the success of my business and that document was my One Page Business Plan!

Educate Advocate Now

Greta Olano
President

ONE
PAGE
PLAN

---

vision

Within the next 3 years grow Educate Advocate Now into a profitable and sustainable local, educational consulting company with annual pre-tax income totaling $150,000 by providing coaching, consulting, and advocacy services for children with AD/HD as well as support and guidance for their families and teachers.

---

mission

Inspiring children with AD/HD to a higher level of personal and academic success.

---

objectives

- Earn pre-tax profits in 2010 of $30,000.
- Earn monthly pre-tax dollars totaling $6,000 in 2010.
- Add 2 new school accounts; each having an est. value of $5,000.
- Have a minimum of 20 parents sign up for each pro bono workshop.
- Increase client retention rate from 80% to 95% by 3rd Qtr. 2010.
- Return new client interest inquiries within 24 hrs. from 48 hrs.
- Write 1 article per qtr. for CHADD organization.
- Take minimum of 3 weeks vacation per year.

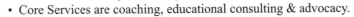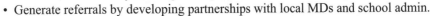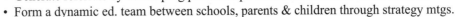
strategies

- Focus on schools by marketing to local PTAs.
- Core Services are coaching, educational consulting & advocacy.
- Promote initial trial by offering value proposition of 1/2 hr free phone consultation.
- Generate referrals by developing partnerships with local MDs and school admin.
- Form a dynamic ed. team between schools, parents & children through strategy mtgs.
- Become local expert in child dev. and AD/HD by obtaining cert. from ACO.
- Generate pro bono AD/HD wkshps to be offered through local PTA.
- Control print & advertise expense by bartering with friends in the print business.

---

action plans

- Initiate Learning Disabilities Focus Study by Jan 15th.
- Launch Pro Bono Parenting Workshops by March 1st.
- Create Educate Advocate tri-fold brochure May 15th.
- Obtain AD/HD coaching cert. from ACO by May 31st.
- Visit local MD's that specialize in AD/HD & schools May - Sept.
- Launch Educate Advocate Website by July 31st.
- Complete Grad School - Educational Therapy by June 2011.

VISION
MISSION
OBJECTIVES
STRATEGIES
ACTION PLANS

Introduction

What is a One Page Business Plan?

*"Planning is a process...
not an event!*

*One Page Plans
are living,
changing,
evolving
documents!"*

The One Page Business Plan is an innovative approach to business planning that captures the essence of any business, project or program on a single page using key words and short phrases.

Most companies use the process to create not only the company's overall plan, but also to create plans for each supporting department, project and program. Since the creation of The One Page Business Plan in 1994, over 500,000 companies have successfully used the process to bring structure, alignment and accountability to their organizations.

The flexible methodology makes it possible for entrepreneurs, business owners, executives, managers and professionals in every organization to have a plan. The standard format makes it easy to review, compare and understand plans.

One Page Business Plans work because:

- Plans actually get documented
- Plans are understandable
- Plans are easy to write, easy to update
- Every manager or team has one

The process creates:

- Alignment
- Accountability
- Results

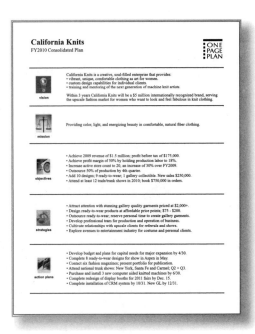

Our Observations...

Why One Page?

You are busy; your time is limited. You want to spend your time in front of prospects and clients, marketing and selling your services. You are action and results oriented. Most of us are not good at prose writing... it takes too long to write a well-written sentence, paragraph, page or chapter - and far too long to read. People need to be able to read a plan in about five minutes. They want the essence... the key points. Then they want to talk... to ask clarifying questions, come to agreement... and then take action.

Why Plan?

Some need to write plans to get funding... however, since few small businesses are fundable other than by friends and family, funding is not the primary reason people write plans. Most people write plans because they either want or need to achieve different or better results. Plans are blueprints; they describe what is going to be built, how it will be done, and by whom... and the results to be measured.

Why Written Plans?

The spoken word is too fluid; we have a tendency to ramble. When we speak, we almost never say it exactly the same way twice... frequently we forget to share some of the most important details... or spend too much time on the unimportant things. When we write, we choose our words more carefully. Writing takes time, usually much more than talk. The written word requires a higher level of mindfulness and attention to detail. The written word also produces a contract with yourself and others that can be reread, refined... a source for reflection and mindful change if necessary.

Asking simple questions works!

People love to talk about their business! They can easily answer questions like, what are you building, what will your practice look like in three years, what has made your business successful to date, what are the critical business development projects and programs you have underway or planned, what do you measure to know if you are on track... and of course, why does your business exist?

The Power is in 5 Key Questions!

Business plan terminology is problematic. Depending on where you went to school, and the companies/organizations you have worked for... the terms Vision, Mission, Objectives, Strategies and Plans probably mean something different to you than the person sitting next to you. We have learned that business planning "definitions" just don't work. We have refined our questions over 15 years with hundreds of thousands of business owners. The five questions we will teach you are simple, easy to remember and they will help get your business plan out of your head and onto paper.

About Planning Processes

Starting with a blank page wastes valuable time!

The examples and the fill-in-the-blank prompts are learning aids... designed to help you quickly learn and master the One Page Business Plan technique. We have learned that most people learn by seeing examples, so we give you lots of them.

The dreaded "writer's block" can easily be eliminated by the use of our proprietary fill-in-the-blank templates. They make the creation of any portion of your business plan easy. Use the fill-in-the-blank templates to quickly capture your thoughts and create the first draft. You will also find that the extensive list of templates can spark your thinking and make sure that you give consideration to your "total" business.

Everyone on your team can and should write a One Page Business Plan!

Have partners? Employees? The number one issue business owners and executives share with us is that they need people to work on the right things... and achieve specific results! Partners complain they are not on the same page! There is a simple solution: have your partners, associates, strategic alliance partners, managers and paid staff create One Page Business Plans for their businesses, profit centers, departments, projects or programs. Do not assume they are executing your plan. Have them create their own!

Final Thought: Plans are important... Execution is critical!

Women in business invest in planning because they want and need results. Plans are valuable because they provide the blueprint for where you are taking your business and how you will get there... but ultimately the plans are only as good as the execution. Establish processes such as the scorecard tracking and monthly progress reviews to monitor the implementation of your plans.

Business Plan Terminology is Confusing

There are no universally acceptable definitions to the terms Vision, Mission, Objectives, Strategies or Action Plans. How you use these terms depends entirely on what school you went to and for what companies you have worked. Many companies never successfully complete their business plans because they cannot agree on the basic terminology. We solved the problem!

We translated the five standard business plan elements into five simple and universal questions:

Vision: What are you building?

Mission: Why does this business exist?

Objectives: What business results will you measure?

Strategies: How will you build this business?

Action Plans: What is the work to be done?

Writing a business plan for a department or program?

Modify the Mission and Strategy questions by replacing the word "business" with "department" or "program":

Department Usage	Program Usage
Mission: Why does this department exist?	Mission: Why does this program exist?
Strategy: How will you build this department?	Strategy: How will you build this program?

Business Plans Can be Simple and Clean

The best way to understand The One Page Business Plan is to read one... One Page Business Plans can generally be read in about five minutes or less.

California Knits
Consolidated Plan
FY2010

 ONE PAGE PLAN

vision

California Knits is a creative, soul-filled enterprise that provides:
• vibrant, unique, comfortable clothing as art for women.
• custom design capabilities for individual clients.
• training and mentoring of the next generation of machine knit artists.

Within 3 years California Knits will be a $5 million internationally recognized brand, serving the upscale fashion market for women who want to look and feel fabulous in knit clothing.

mission

Providing color, light, and energizing beauty in comfortable, natural fiber clothing.

objectives

• Achieve 2010 revenue of $1.5 million; profit before tax of $175,000.
• Achieve profit margin of 50% by holding production labor to 18%.
• Increase active store count to 20, an increase of 30% over FY2009.
• Outsource 50% of production by 4th quarter.
• Add 10 designs; 9 ready-to-wear; 1 gallery collectible. New sales $250,000.
• Attend at least 12 trade/trunk shows in 2010; book $750,000 in orders.

strategies

• Attract attention with stunning gallery quality garments priced at $2,000+.
• Design ready-to-wear products at affordable price points; $75 - $200.
• Outsource ready-to-wear; reserve personal time to create gallery garments.
• Develop professional team for production and operation of business.
• Cultivate relationships with upscale clients for referrals and shows.
• Explore avenues to entertainment industry for costume and personal clients.

action plans

• Develop budget and plans for capital needs for major expansion by 4/30.
• Complete 8 ready-to-wear designs for show in Aspen in May.
• Contact six fashion magazines; present portfolio for publication.
• Attend national trunk shows: New York, Santa Fe and Carmel; Q2 + Q3.
• Purchase and install 3 new computer aided knitting machines by 6/30.
• Complete redesign of display booths for 2011 fairs by Dec. 15.
• Complete installation of CRM system by 10/31. New GL by 12/31.

The One Page Business Plan has Many Uses

Planning Process

- Annual business plan
- Executive summary for large organizations
- Project & program plan development
- Plans for support & administrative functions
- Solid basis for developing budgets

External Presentations

- Executive summary for bank/other funders
- Strategic alliances
- Board and volunteer recruitment (non-profits)
- Strategic hires
- Advocacy

Brainstorming

- Process for brainstorming business, products or programs
- Initial draft for new programs
- Framework for potential expansion
- Pro forma for mergers & acquisition
- "What if" for downsizing & restructuring

Process and Performance Management

- Professional & leadership development
- Framework for compensation systems
- Clear structure for measuring outcomes
- Benchmark to measure progress against priorities
- Improve cross-functional communications
- Creates culture of accountability & responsibility

How to Use This Book and CD

The primary purpose of this book is to help you get your plan onto paper. It has been carefully crafted to capture the plan that is in your head.

Carry this book with you, write in it, use it as a container for capturing your thoughts as they occur. If you have multiple businesses, partners or managers, have them get their own copy.

It's not necessary to do all the exercises in this book. If you can write your One Page Business Plan by reviewing the samples — skip the exercises. They are there to help guide you through the process if you need help.

This book does not look like the typical business planning book — it isn't intended to. The exercises and examples are meant to stimulate you. The graphics and images are meant to guide you. If they look playful, be playful and explore. If they look analytical, be analytical and focused. The examples and samples are from real business plans. They are meant to show you how powerful a few words or a well-constructed phrase can be.

Do not underestimate the power of the questions that appear simple! They are simple by design. If you do not get an "aha" from them, have somebody ask you the questions. Important insights may begin to flow.

This book is divided into nine sections with the focus on the five elements of The One Page Business Plan. You can start anywhere. It's OK to jump around!

There are many different ways to use and interact with this book. Exercises can be done:

- by oneself

- with a planning partner (2 or more women in business)

- as a management team

- as a group

- at a retreat or conference

- with a licensed One Page Business Plan consultant

The Women in Business Tool Kit CD at the back of the book contains The One Page Business Plan templates, bonus exercises, budget worksheet, plus scorecards for monitoring and tracking your results.

VISION
MISSION
OBJECTIVES
STRATEGIES
ACTION PLANS

Assessments

What's working? What's not?

> *"Too many people over plan and under execute.*
>
> *Plan for what is critical… then execute your plan."*

Intuitively you know the status of your business, profit center, project or program… but when was the last time you stopped and gave it a checkup? Took a real look under the hood?

This section has two 10 Point Assessments to help you quickly determine what is working in your company, and what isn't. We've also included a 10 Point Personal Assessment for you to do a little personal checkup, if you so desire.

These assessments are designed to help you quickly take the pulse of your business, which areas are strong, which aspects need attention. As with all of the exercises in this book, they are meant to be done quickly, relying on your intuition, state of mind and frankly, what is keeping you up at night and/or making you smile.

We encourage you not to overwork these assessments. In our workshops we give participants about five minutes to do the overall business assessment.

It's possible that not all of the categories on the 10 Point Assessments will apply to your business; if so, you have two choices: 1) ignore those that do not apply; 2) modify the category to reflect an area of your business that is critical to your success and then rate your performance.

As you work through your plan, be sure to come back to these assessments to ensure your plan addresses the key issues you identify here.

What's Working in Your Business? What's Not?

Step 1: Rate each of these elements on a scale of 1 to 10; 1 = disaster, 10 = brilliantly successful
Step 2: On page 31 identify the key elements/issues that influenced your rating.
Step 3: On page 31 make note of what needs to be changed to correct the problem areas.

	N/A	1	2	3	4	5	6	7	8	9	10
1. Sales	N/A	1	2	3	4	5	6	7	8	9	10
2. Profitability	N/A	1	2	3	4	5	6	7	8	9	10
3. Cash Flow	N/A	1	2	3	4	5	6	7	8	9	10
4. Planning & Budgets	N/A	1	2	3	4	5	6	7	8	9	10
5. Expense Control	N/A	1	2	3	4	5	6	7	8	9	10
6. Marketing & New Products	N/A	1	2	3	4	5	6	7	8	9	10
7. Technology	N/A	1	2	3	4	5	6	7	8	9	10
8. Employees & Subcontractors	N/A	1	2	3	4	5	6	7	8	9	10
9. Strategic Alliances/Vendors	N/A	1	2	3	4	5	6	7	8	9	10
10. Quality & Safety	N/A	1	2	3	4	5	6	7	8	9	10
Overall Assessment		**1**	**2**	**3**	**4**	**5**	**6**	**7**	**8**	**9**	**10**

Step 4: As you develop your plan, be sure to come back to this page to address the issues identified here.

THE ONE PAGE BUSINESS PLAN

Where are the Opportunities for Improvement?

In left column: Identify key issues or opportunities that influenced your assessment.
In right column: Brainstorm actions that can be taken to improve low ratings or maintain high ratings.

Key Issue or Opportunity	Action to Improve or Maintain
Example: Poor Sales	More phone contact with existing clients, less emphasis on collateral, more listening, offer better solutions

Your Sales/Marketing Programs: What's Working?

Step 1: Rate each of these elements on a scale of 1 to 10; 1 = disaster, 10 = brilliantly successful
Step 2: On page 33 identify the key elements/issues that influenced your rating.
Step 3: On page 33 make note of what needs to be changed to correct the problem areas.

1. Know & Understand our Ideal Client	N/A	1	2	3	4	5	6	7	8	9	10
2. Compelling Product & Service Offerings	N/A	1	2	3	4	5	6	7	8	9	10
3. Effective Marketing System that Attracts our Ideal Clients	N/A	1	2	3	4	5	6	7	8	9	10
4. Pricing Policies that Attract Ideal Clients & Produce Excellent Margins	N/A	1	2	3	4	5	6	7	8	9	10
5. Effective Customer Service Systems	N/A	1	2	3	4	5	6	7	8	9	10
6. Strong Strategic Alliances	N/A	1	2	3	4	5	6	7	8	9	10
7. Effective Advertising, Promotions, Events, Seminars	N/A	1	2	3	4	5	6	7	8	9	10
8. Compelling Web Site & Collateral Materials	N/A	1	2	3	4	5	6	7	8	9	10
9. Sales & Marketing Activity Tracking Systems	N/A	1	2	3	4	5	6	7	8	9	10
10. Effective Project & Cost Controls	N/A	1	2	3	4	5	6	7	8	9	10
Overall Assessment		1	2	3	4	5	6	7	8	9	10

Step 4: As you develop your plan, be sure to come back to this page to address the issues identified here.

Where are the Opportunities for Improvement?

In left column: Identify key issues or opportunities that influenced your assessment.
In right column: Brainstorm actions that can be taken to improve low ratings or maintain high ratings.

Key Issue or Opportunity	Action to Improve or Maintain

Example for Advertising, Promos, Events: Local advertising and promotions producing too few leads	Move to more personal forms of business development like seminars & special events. More contact with existing customers

How are you? A Personal Assessment

Step 1: Rate each of these elements on a scale of 1 to 10; 1 = disaster, 10 = brilliantly successful
Step 2: On page 35 identify the key elements/issues that influenced your rating.
Step 3: On page 35 make note of what needs to be changed to correct the problem areas.

1. Your Physical Health	N/A	1	2	3	4	5	6	7	8	9	10
2. Your Mental Health	N/A	1	2	3	4	5	6	7	8	9	10
3. Relationships at Work	N/A	1	2	3	4	5	6	7	8	9	10
4. Your Role at Work	N/A	1	2	3	4	5	6	7	8	9	10
5. Personal Finances	N/A	1	2	3	4	5	6	7	8	9	10
6. Life Outside of Work	N/A	1	2	3	4	5	6	7	8	9	10
7. Sense of Community	N/A	1	2	3	4	5	6	7	8	9	10
8. Plans for Retirement	N/A	1	2	3	4	5	6	7	8	9	10
9. Stress Level	N/A	1	2	3	4	5	6	7	8	9	10
10. Sense of Well Being	N/A	1	2	3	4	5	6	7	8	9	10
Overall Assessment		**1**	**2**	**3**	**4**	**5**	**6**	**7**	**8**	**9**	**10**

Step 4: As you develop your plan, be sure to come back to this page to address the issues identified here.

Where are the Opportunities for Improvement?

In left column: Identify key issues or opportunities that influenced your assessment.
In right column: Brainstorm actions that can be taken to improve low ratings or maintain high ratings.

Key Issue or Opportunity	Action to Improve or Maintain

| **Example for Life Outside Work:**

Not having enough fun! Need some downtime! | Consider taking Mondays off, or every other Monday. Need time to rejuvenate. Spend time on the boat with family. |

The Vision Statement

What are you building?

"If you don't get the words right...

you might build the wrong business!"

Everybody is building something... a company, an organization, a department, professional practice, a non-profit*. Well-written Vision Statements answer the question: What is being built?... in three sentences or less!

The question for you is what are you building? What do you want your business to look like in 1, 3 or 5 years? An effective Vision Statement need not be long, but it must clearly describe what you are building. A few key words will go a long way.

Vision Statements answer these questions:

- What type of business is this?
- What markets does it serve?
- What is the geographic scope?
- Where will the business be located?
- Who are the target customers?
- What are the key products and services?
- How big will the company be... and when?
- What will revenues be?
- Will it have employees? How many?

Almost everyone has a Vision for their company, but some are better at articulating it. Many people struggle with capturing their Vision effectively in writing. At The One Page Business Plan Company we have learned that with a little prompting, most entrepreneurs, business professionals, executives and owners can capture the essence of their Vision in just a few minutes.

If you are building a non-profit you will find The One Page Business Plan for Non-Profit Organizations to be very helpful. This book was created specifically for non-profits and is full of non-profit sample plans.

A Simple Formula for Writing a Vision Statement...

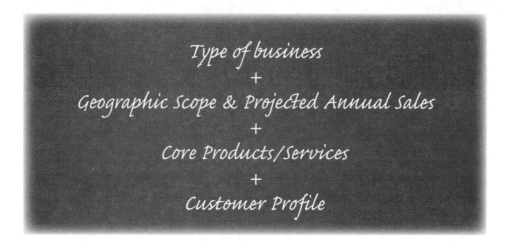

Type of business
+
Geographic Scope & Projected Annual Sales
+
Core Products/Services
+
Customer Profile

Here are some examples using this formula:

Ezme Designs	Within the next 5 years, grow Ezme Designs into a successful international ceramics, housewares and lifestyle company, with annual sales of $250,000 providing unique, handmade, quality designs of tableware, jewelry and sculptural ceramics to art conscious men and women, retail stores, catalogs, craft galleries and internet shoppers.
Harps, Etc.	Within the next 3 years grow Harps, Etc. into a $2 million international harp sales and accessories retail company providing new and used harps for sales, rental and instruction, plus accessories and services to professionals, students, teachers and aficionados of the harp.
Suit Your Fancy	Within the next 2 years grow Suit Your Fancy into a $50,000, successful national home-based party-plan retail sales business providing high quality stylish and comfortable women's clothing and offering valuable entrepreneurial opportunities to incredibly motivated women in all ages and stages of life desiring to create their own business successes.
East Bay Yoga	Within the next 3 years grow East Bay Yoga into a $100,000 San Francisco Bay Area provider of on-site workplace yoga classes, inspiring companies and their employees to create a satisfying and fulfilling work/life experience by transforming their moment-to-moment awareness. We will also create and sell new yoga-related DVDs locally and online to support the ongoing practice of living life more fully through yoga.

 **Crafting a Vision Statement**

Getting the first draft onto paper is always the most difficult. It is infinitely easier to edit! The fill-in-the-blank-template below is geared to help you quickly create a first draft. Each blank in essence is a question; complete all the blanks, and you create a first draft... quickly and easily! Not able to fill in all of the blanks at this time? Don't worry... complete those that you can! Revisit the blanks later, you may need to do some research or enlist help from others.

Vision Statement

Within the next _____ years grow _____ into a $_____
                             (company name)   (est. annual sales)

_____ _____ company providing
    (geographic scope)   (type of business)
    (local/region/nat'l/int'l)

_____
               (list 2-3 of your most successful products/services)

to _____
        (list 2-3 characteristics of your ideal clients/customers)

The following Vision Statement was created using the fill-in-the-blanks template and then edited. It is brief, but very clear.

"Within the next <u>3</u> years grow <u>Roberta Jones' practice at Boston Financial Advisory Services</u> into a <u>regional</u> <u>financial advisory practice managing $40 million in assets yielding at least $350,000 in gross revenue</u> specializing in <u>plan development and asset management</u> for <u>professional working women age 30 to 60 who want to be financially prepared for retirement</u>."

This exercise is designed to help you brainstorm the Who, What, Why, When, Where and Hows for your business. Review the questions, write down your initial thoughts, insights and ahas. Writing outside the boxes is allowed and encouraged.

WHAT?

Services or products? or both? How many?

Company image: What will this company be known for?

Owner's Role: What is your role? How will you spend your time?

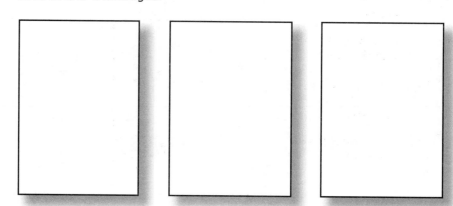

WHERE?

Company: Local, regional, national, or international?

Clients/Recipients: Where are they? What cities, states, countries?

Business Operations: Headquarters, offices, program locations, etc.?

WHO?

Customers: Who are they? What needs do they have?

Staff: Who needs to be on your team? When

Strategic Alliances: Who can you partner with?

Advisors: Who can provide professional and strategic advice and help you grow this business properly?

Creating the Business You Want

Don't worry about answering all of the questions; they may or may not apply to your business.

WHEN?

Start-up: When will this business be operational?

Facilities: When will office/manufacturing/distribution space be required?

Systems: When must they be selected, tested, and operational?

WHY?

Owner: Why am I creating this business?

Customers/Clients: Why will they buy these products or services?

Investors/Bankers: Why will they fund this business?

HOW?

Funding: How will this business be funded?

Culture: How do you want to interact with customers, employees, vendors?

Personal Beliefs: How will your personal beliefs impact this business?

Crafting a Vision Statement for a Department*

If your company has support functions, have each of your managers create a Vision Statement for their department. This template will make creating the first draft easy.

Department Vision Statement Template

Within the next _____ years grow _____ at _____
       (1, 3, or 5 yrs)   (department name)   (company name)

into a successful provider of _____
                         (describe services and/or functions)

to _____. Future capabilities/capacity
      (name internal/external customers)

will include _____.
                 (describe capabilities/capacity)

Example

Marketing Team at Unity in Marin Spiritual Center

Within the next <u>3 years</u> develop the <u>Marketing Team</u> at <u>Unity In Marin</u> into a highly efficient and effective volunteer marketing team that provides <u>pro bono services in marketing, advertising, public relations, promotions and special events services</u> to <u>support programs and events identified by the Board of Directors and other committees.</u>

*For larger/established companies

Department Vision Statements that Work Together

Well written Vision Statements at the department level answer the question, "What will this department look like in 1, 3, or 5 years?" The Vision Statements should provide a sense of the services and/or function that the department will be providing within the planning horizon indicated.

Here is an example of a set of integrated Vision Statements for one company:

Consolidated Plan	Within the next 3 years, build a $150 million global wireless applications solutions company serving the financial services, health care and transportation industries.
Sales	Within the next 18 months, build a national external sales department consisting of 20 senior sales reps focused on large custom system sales supported by a highly effective telemarketing function with 6 specialists selling packaged products & limited consulting services.
Marketing	Over the next 3 years, expand Marketing to include market research, product development & marketing communications depts.; total staff: 10 professionals + 5 support. Continue to outsource PR & Advertising.
Engineering & Technology	Over the next 3 years, build a state-of-the-art technology center with an engineering team of 30 professionals capable of designing, building, & hosting leading edge wireless products and services.
Human Resources	Build a highly motivated and effective global workforce of non-union employees and independent contractors to support a rapidly growing company. Internal HR staff will consist of 6 employees.
Accounting & Finance	Build highly efficient accounting system/function that seamlessly integrates all of the business' financial, operational, customer & management processes. Total head count in 3 years of 20.

The Vision Statement... as Tamara Sees It

Vision answers the question, "What are you building?" It is a statement that creates a picture, with words, of the design and structure of your business.

The best part of putting your vision in writing now is that it marks the starting point of what your idea looks like at this given moment. It will surprise you to see how it will change. Your vision captures your creativity and becomes a record of the journey your business will take and also reflects your personal growth over time.

Initially my vision began with a small picture and then quickly developed into something much larger. The beauty is that your vision expands and grows as you do. My first One Page Business Plan was written when I was developing my first product idea, the TP Saver®, a product that prevents toddlers and pets from unrolling the toilet paper. My vision at that time was written to describe a "single product company that sold the product through retail stores to families." A few months later, as women asked me to produce their products for them my "vision" expanded to include production of other "Mom Invented" products. Therefore, I had to revise my own plan to encompass this much broader vision to "Within three years Mom Inventors, Inc. will manufacture and distribute a line of juvenile products under the internationally trademarked Mom Invented® brand through the nation's top retailers..." And, with my focus on building a community and offering business resources, my vision has substantially changed since the original draft and continues to expand and evolve.

When you first come up with your business idea, it is important to let the idea percolate in your mind and brainstorm about all the possibilities. As your thinking takes shape it becomes essential to discover the specific words to describe what your business will look like. Imagine an architect who first sketches out the fundamental designs and structures of a new building on paper. Like an architect, this process will help you narrow your focus, gain clarity about what you intend to create, and sketches out the parameters from which to work.

A common mistake that I find is that often our vision is either too vague or broad in scope. For example, I worked with an intelligent woman this year whose initial vision described the actual construction of a complex, high tech building she planned to build as an arts facility for youth. However, by the end of the process she came to realize that she didn't want to construct a building, but instead wanted to create a program for kids. Once that became clear, finding an adequate facility was merely an action step. Therefore, when writing your vision, ask yourself, "Is this describing precisely what I am building?"

Sage Advice on Vision Statements

Your business is a very personal journey

My work by it's nature, has been a very personal journey. I have come to understand who I am as a woman through my business. I always knew who I was as a woman, daughter, wife and friend, but in business I have become me, independently. I have come into my full creative self, learned to express my power, learned when to let the power position go and learned how to get things done without taking advantage of anything female...just by being a good honest business person. I am at a place where the jobs I don't take are as important as the ones I do. I am very proud of what I have done and it's a great feeling.

April Sheldon, Interior Designer, Founder
April Sheldon Design
www.aprilsheldondesign.com

Most businesses take 3 – 5 years to break even

Building your own business takes an incredible amount of commitment, both to yourself and to your idea. It's one thing to follow the adrenaline rush to bring your idea to market, which may last 3-6 months until you launch the business. It's quite a different undertaking to have this same level of energy 1, 2 and three years into it. Are you OK with no vacations for the next 3 years and eating proverbial peanut butter and jelly sandwiches instead of going out to eat? Most businesses take 3-5 years to break even, and there are very few businesses that are successful without considerable time and effort. Starting your own business will teach you more about yourself than anything else you've ever done: college, graduate degrees, your latest job. You will grow and expand your mind and you will always know, " I did it!". It's incredibly empowering. If you've picked the right business to start, you will never dread going to work, again.

Cathy Bennett, Founder
How Fast Time Flies™
www.howfasttimeflies.com

Build your business by choosing who you want to work with!

I picked my target audience simply by choosing the kind of people I wanted to work with the most: mompreneurs. Then I brainstormed like crazy on questions like: "What do mompreneurs need? What's their biggest challenge? What is not working for them right now? What would make their life better/simpler/happier?" Then I set about finding out the answers, which I then used to create my programs and products. My business has really taken off and my pipeline remains full of qualified prospects because I've tailored my offerings to be solutions to my target market's problems.

Lara Galloway
The Mom Biz Coach
www.mombizcoach.com

Sage Advice on Vision Statements

Selling my business was the best thing I ever did

The hardest decision I ever made was to sell my business. When I first started the Metronome Ballroom, it felt like "I had to do it or die." Admitting that the burning desire to build and run my business was turning into burn out, was hard to face. But I learned that you can only bury the truth for so long. Selling my business was the best thing I ever did, because it opened the doors for opening a new business, the Ballroom Dance Teachers College. With this new business I used my skills and experience to build a national organization and to make a much bigger impact on my industry. I was also able to design this business to accommodate a lifestyle that had become important to me. I learned that it is not failure to sell a business you have created, but rather a closing of a chapter that has come to its natural end, so as to start a new one.

Diane Jarmolow (Former Owner/Director, Metronome Ballroom, San Francisco)
Founder and Director, Ballroom Dance Teachers College
www.teachballroomdancing.com

Entreprenuership or Employment? Make the right decision!

I created my own business that was problematic, but ultimately successful and rewarding. What I didn't realize until the end were two things: First, I really didn't have the administrative skills initially to run a business, making it particularly difficult when the business took off (my clients were Fortune 500 companies). Second, working for a well-established firm can have enormous benefits as well. Making the right choice up front is crucial. My friend Cindy got a job in high school at a grocery chain as a cashier. While the rest of us went off to college, she stayed with that company. Decades later, she is happy, has great benefits and still works there. I am proud of what I have done, but next time I would focus more carefully on my weaknesses in order to make my path easier or... I would take Cindy's path instead.

Dana Dworin, Realtor
Pacific Union
www.pacunion.com/danadworin

Vision enrolls and excites the passion in others... and you

Vision! It is a compelling picture of a future possibility of what can be. It pulls you from the inside out, stretching and yet challenging your imagination. You can taste it, smell it, feel it – like a tingle of goose bumps providing a large dose of OMG excitement. When a vision is articulated to others, it enrolls and excites them in a favorable way that aligns with their values and passions. Like the scene in the movie when Harry met Sally, the restaurant patron said: "I'll have what she's having." It is essential to have a clear compelling vision of what the future possibility can be for your venture. Tap in, tune in, and turn on your imagination – that's where your vision lives. And don't allow border bullies or naysayers to plop boulders on your path!

Dory Willer, SPHR, PCC, 2003 International Coach of the Year
Beacon Quest Coaching
www.BeaconQuest.com

Next Steps for Your Vision Statement

1 **REVIEW:** Does your Vision Statement answer these questions?

VISION STATEMENT QUESTIONS:	YES/NO
What type of business is this?	
What markets does it serve?	
What is the geographic scope?	
Where will the business be located?	
Who are the target customers?	
What are the key products and services?	
How big will the company be... and when?	
What will revenues be?	
Will it have employees? How many?	

2 **REFLECT:** Assuming the reader knows nothing about your business, does your Vision Statement clearly answer the question: *What are you building? Ask yourself... Is this the business I want to build?*

3 **SHARE:** After reflecting on your Vision Statement for a few days, consider sharing your Vision Statement with at least a couple of people and asking them for feedback.

4 **COMPLETION!:** Satisfied with your Vision Statement? Go to the CD at the back of the book, find The One Page Business Plan template in the Forms and Templates folder, and type your Vision Statement into the template.

VISION

MISSION

OBJECTIVES

STRATEGIES

ACTION PLANS

Mission

Why does this business exist?

Mission Statements always answer the question, "Who will we serve and what will we do for them?"

Every company exists for a reason. Good Mission Statements describe why your product, service, department, project, program or business exists. Great Mission Statements are short and memorable. They communicate in just a few words (8 words are ideal) the company's focus and what is being provided to customers. They always answer the question, "Why will customers buy this product or service?"

Some of the best Mission Statements are an integral part of a company's branding strategy that compels customers to buy, but the same Mission Statements can and do direct and influence all significant business and management decisions.

It is critical to have a Mission Statement that speaks to your ideal client... and to you. If your business is built to provide practical home products for families with children under the age of 5, your Mission Statement should speak to them. If your ideal client is a high net worth executive in her early fifties, you must have a Mission Statement that attracts her. Creating fashion products for professional women in their thirties? Young couples just starting their careers? Businesses with 50–500 employees? Grandparents? You must have a Mission Statement that explains in 8–12 words how your products or services improve their lives.

Mission Statements answer these specific questions:

- Why does this business exist?
- What are we committed to providing to our customers?
- What promise are we making to our clients?
- What wants, needs, desires, pain or problems do our product/services solve?
- What is our unique selling proposition?

A Simple Formula for Writing a Mission Statement...

> *Ideal Client Description*
> *+*
> *Goal/Benefit of your Products/Services*

Here are some examples using this formula:

IM Solutions	We help businesses strategize & implement their online marketing.
Tamura Insurance	Building, growing and protecting your family's financial legacy.
Chemarci	Our imported Italian products capture the essence of La Dolce Vita.
Above & Beyond Concierge Services	We help Seniors and families design critical document storage systems... creating priceless peace of mind.
The Quantum Business	We help smart people work better together.
Crime Site Cleanup Company	We do for families what no one should ever have to do.
Bhurji Indian Grocery Store	We bring the taste of India to your home.
The ShortCut Cooks	We are on a mission to rescue people from heavy kitchen duty.
Sarah Oliver Handbags	We provide fashion conscious women with fabulously sophisticated handbags that have an inspiring and heartfelt story.

Crafting Your Mission Statement

Use the fill-in-the-blank template below to create a first draft of your Mission Statement. Experiment with variations until you come up with a short, powerful, memorable statement that describes your ideal clients and how you serve them. The best Mission Statements are 8-12 words.

Why does this business exist?

1st Attempt:

We help _____ _____.
      (recipient of your products/services)   (goal or benefit of your products/services)

2nd Attempt:

3rd Attempt:

Believe it or not... you have a choice as to who you work with! Consider these questions:

- Who do you want to work with?
- What causes/issues are important to you?
- What problems can you solve?
- Who is currently working with your ideal client?

- Where are the people you want to serve?
- What work gives you professional satisfaction?
- Who has the resources to pay your fees?
- Who makes you smile?

Exercise instructions:

1. In the center circle, describe the people, groups or organizations you want to work with. These people have faces! What do they look like? What do they need help with? The more specific you can be... the easier it will be for you to find them, and vice-versa.

2. In the outer circle, list the people and/or communities that know your existing and/or future clients. These people need to know you exist; they can introduce you to those that need your service.

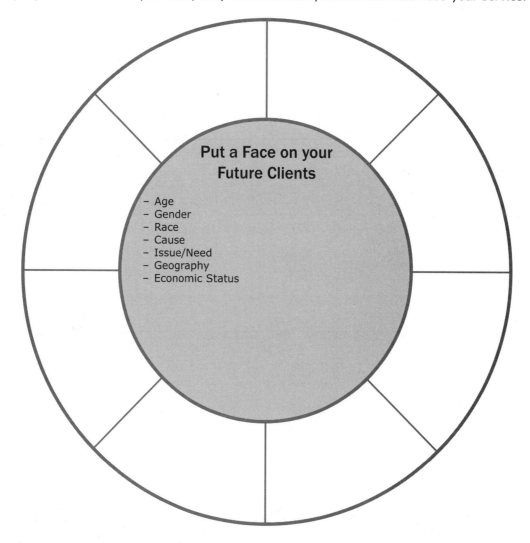

When you are clear about who you want to serve, you make it easier for them to find you!

And Why?

Why will clients/recipients use/buy your services/products? What value do these services or products provide the client? What unique benefits do these services or products provide the client/recipient?

What passion(s) are you trying to satisfy by building this business? What beliefs do you have about your products/services that are driving you to create/grow this business? What is the highest good that this business can achieve? What values will drive you? Who will benefit from your work?

The Mission Statement... as Tamara Sees It

I like to think of the mission as the "heart" of your business. The mission answers the question why does this business exist, and more specifically what is the promise you are making to your customers or clients.

Perhaps the most essential component, and greatest challenge, of the mission statement is brevity. This is the phrase that must glide off your tongue every time you are asked the question, "What do you do?" It must be clear, concise, and impactful. It is best if it can create a "wow" factor letting your passion come across and inspire others.

My own two-part mission (there are two parts to my business) remains a work in progress:

For the online and educational portion of my business, the mission is to...

> *"Inspire, inform & boldly promote courageous women in business"*

And...

For the consumer products side of my business, the mission is to...

> *"Celebrate the creativity of moms by launching innovative Mom Invented® products around the world."*

After you have gone through a few drafts and think you are getting close, test it. Have a friend ask, "So, what do you do?" Your answer is your mission statement. After you answer, ask your friend if it was clear and how it made her feel about your business. When you recite your mission it should feel good to you, make sense to them, and have a strong and memorable impact.

At this point, you need to do another test by asking yourself if your "mission" supports your "vision". If it does not, revise one or both until it does.

It's important to get the mission "right" so it is worth the effort. Your business will demand a tremendous amount of your time and energy. Your mission reflects your heart and passion. Getting the mission "right" puts you in accordance with your internal compass. This compass is at the core of who you are, will help you stay the course even in tumultuous times, and will guide you on your journey to business success.

Sage Advice on Mission Statements

Have a laser focus on your ideal client! Say no to others.

When I started my natural fiber clothing company for plus size women, I knew exactly who my target market was. It was not women who "thought" they were fat, it was women who knew they were fat and they knew this because they couldn't find any nice, attractive, or well made clothing that fit them. When we got requests from smaller women to please make clothing in their size, I politely referred them to other sources. We had a mission and we were not to be distracted. This laser focus was instrumental to our success.

Cynthia Riggs (Founder and Former Owner, Making it Big, Inc.)
President, Women Building Business
www.womenbuildingbusiness.com

Being "human" is the cornerstone of building a successful business

I always heard "Business is business"... which led me to believe that the "human" aspect of business was less important. What I've learned along the way, is that being "human" is the cornerstone of building a successful business. Work with integrity. Treat people right, customers and employees. Do the right thing, even when no one is watching. These tenets, coupled with a strong plan and effective execution, will create your success!

Gwen Gallagher
President, Old Republic Home Protection
www.orhp.com

Own Your Power

No matter what your role, you have power. You have power to influence situations, make decisions, set direction, and respond appropriately. No matter who you are. It's always up to you to step up and own your power by using a proactive approach. Successful women have the word "initiative" as their middle name.

Luanne Stevenson
Pajaro Group Consulting, Inc.
www.pajarogroupconsulting.com

Your mission is important, invest in skills you don't have

None of us have all of the skills we need to build and grow our business. For most of my career I have had the philosophy that I must have a business intelligence team that provides the knowledge, resources, know-how that I do not have. I encourage you to compliment and invest in a team that helps you fill in the blanks. Your business will be smarter, grow faster, be more profitable. You will sleep better at night.

Pat Poyle (former Advertising Director, Saturn Division, General Motors)
President, Henry Business Solutions
www.henrysolutions.net

Sage Advice on Mission Statements

Your plan must support your life priorities

As a woman in business, it is especially important that you create your business plan to support your life priorities. In order to do this, you must first define success for yourself based on the various stages of your life (completion of school, starting business, getting married, having children, business growing, getting divorced, children in school, children moving out, etc.) As the stages change, there's a good chance your priorities will shift as well. Along the way, remember to revisit and adjust your business plan to best support your definition of success and your priorities for that stage of your life. When our plan and our priorities are aligned, we are better able to achieve success with sanity... in our personal and our professional lives!

Nicola Ries Taggart
The Executive Moms Coach
www.executivemomscoach.com

Always err on the side of generosity

In business when there are disagreements, there is always a choice between being tough and hard vs erring on the side of generosity. I learned when I choose being tough it led to contraction, withholding, tightness, constriction and pain. Conversely, I found if I could just begin inching towards generosity and be more careful in my listening, I created trust which led to solutions and new business that I never could have imagined.

Patrice Wynne, Founder
San Miguel Designs (formerly founder/owner Gaia Bookstore)
www.sanmigueldesigns.com

Creative workforce; Surround yourself with good people

As the popularity for Sarah Oliver Handbags grew, it became impossible for Sarah alone to produce enough bags to meet the surging demand from Gumps and other high-end fashion retailers. Unwilling to abandon her signature care and attention to detail, she sought out a group of skilled knitters who could produce the bags with the same quality that her customers had come to expect. Sarah recruited her team at The Redwoods Community of Seniors in Mill Valley, California, where an incredible group of women – average age 88 – have found new friendships and new meaning for their talents. Sarah's advice: Work with what's in front of you. Share your story every day. Believe in yourself!

Sarah Oliver, Artist, Owner
sarah oliver handbags
www.saraholiverhandbags.com

Next Steps for Your Mission Statement

1 **REVIEW:** Does your Mission Statement answer these questions?

MISSION STATEMENT QUESTIONS:	YES/NO
Who will we serve?	
What are we committed to providing?	
What promise are we making?	
Describe the wants, needs, desires or problems our product/services solve?	

2 **REFLECT:** Assuming the reader knows nothing about your business, does your Mission Statement clearly answer the question: *Why does this business exist? Is it compelling? Does it truly describe why you are building this business?*

3 **SHARE:** After reflecting on your Mission Statement for a few days, consider sharing your Mission Statement with at least a couple of people and asking them for feedback.

4 **COMPLETION!:** Satisfied with your Mission Statement? Go to the CD at the back of the book, find The One Page Business Plan template in the Forms and Templates folder, and type your Mission Statement into the template.

VISION
MISSION
OBJECTIVES
STRATEGIES
ACTION PLANS

Objectives

What business results will be measured?

"Be specific in your goal-setting!

Use your goals to drive your behavior!"

Objectives are short statements that define business success. Good Objectives are easy to write and are instantly recognizable. They answer the question "What business results will we measure?"

Objectives clarify the business results you want or need to accomplish in specific, measurable terms. For an Objective to be effective, it needs to be a well-defined target, outcome or result that can be charted or graphed over time. It is important to include different types of Objectives that cover the entire scope of your business.

Well-conceived Objectives:

- Provide a quantitative pulse of the business
- Focus resources towards specific results
- Define success in a measurable manner
- Give people/organizations specific targets
- Establish a framework for accountability and incentive pay
- Minimize subjectivity and emotionalism
- Measure the end results of work effort

Although there is no magical number of Objectives, a One Page Business Plan can accommodate nine. Consider two to three Objectives for sales or revenue, one for profitability, two or three for marketing and one or two that are process oriented.

A Simple Formula for Writing Objectives...

Action to be Taken
+
Graphable Result
+
Completion Date

Here are some examples using this formula:

- Increase Sales from $1.2 million to $3.0 million over the next three years.

- Achieve Profit before Tax of $450,000 in this fiscal year.

- Reduce Cost of Goods Sold from 43% to 38% of Sales by June 30th.

- Increase monthly units sold from 500 to 750 by August 30th.

- Increase billable hours from 60 to 75 per month by September 30th.

- Increase # of active clients from 46 to 60 by year end.

- Add 110 new clients this year; 40 in 1st half, 30 in Q3 & 40 in Q4.

- Increase average sales ticket from $5.25 per customer to $7.10 by Nov. 15th.

- Reduce Credit Line from $350,000 to $150,000 over the next 120 days.

- Decrease average shipping time from 5 days to 3 days by October 31st.

- Reduce employee turnover from 22% to less than 10% by 6/30.

- Increase percent of internal promotions from 10% to 20% over next two years.

It's easy to craft meaningful Objectives when you use these 5 simple guidelines:

- Objectives are GRAPHABLE BUSINESS RESULTS.

- Include numerical value in every Objective (note, not all Objectives are dollars).

- Use of "from _____ to _____" statements helps to give time & growth perspective.

- Assign a name (when appropriate) & date to assure accountability.

- Objectives included in your One Page Plan are most critical to your success.

Numbers within Numbers

Making sense of the all of the numbers within your business can be very challenging. Setting objectives and goals for the critical results in your business like sales, number of customers and profit, is difficult for most of us

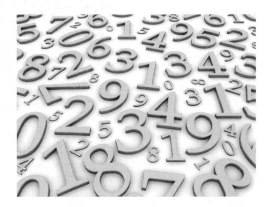

So let's make it simple! In your business you have Activities and Outcomes. If you want to achieve a particular goal, you must do something (Activity). Each of those activities has a result. Let's call those Outcomes. Define the right set of Activities and their Outcomes for your business and you have formulated your recipe for success. You have also defined the right work to be done!

I call this the process of defining the "numbers within numbers". Every critical number or result in your business is a combination of other numbers. These numbers are almost always a combination of activities and outcomes.

In setting goals or objectives you have three choices. You can set goals for 1) activities, 2) outcomes or 3) results (activity count x outcome/activity). As you review the sample plans throughout this book you will see they are generally a combination of activities, outcomes and final results.

Let's look at the numbers within numbers for sales as an example. There are number of transactions, units sold, retail price, discounts, etc. Then there are the number of stores, websites, sales associates, wholesalers and distributors who are actually making the sales.

Stuck? Having trouble estimating sales for next year? Or in 3 to 5 years? Here is a real story about how applying the concept of "numbers within numbers" worked:

> Clarine Hardesty (see page 12) was struggling with estimating how big her gourmet food company would be in five years. When I asked her to estimate sales for this year she intuitively took the number of stores her products are in and multiplied by the average sales per store per month times 12. (16 stores x $2,000/store/year). Then I asked how many stores could she envision her products being in at the end of five years. She said she did not know. I asked is 10,000 stores possible, the instant response was No! 5,000 stores? No! 1,000 stores? No! 500 stores? Response was maybe. 250 stores? That sounded doable. 250 stores x $2,000 per store = $500,000. That is the number Clarine decided made sense to include in her Vision Statement...at this time. Obviously over time it will get refined.

In Clarine's case, her two critical "numbers within numbers" for sales are the number of stores and average monthly sales per store. Much of her plan revolves around these two numbers.

If you get stuck or confused estimating any of the critical numbers in your business, stop... then begin thinking about the numbers within the number you are trying to estimate. Break the critical number into 1) activities and 2) outcomes. Test out various values on the activities and outcomes until you feel your estimate is pretty good. This is not guessing, this is estimating the way the pros do it. Try it, over time it will become much more natural and you will become a lot more confident about your numbers.

Objectives Must be Graphable

The One Page methodology makes writing Objectives simple: All Objectives must be graphable!

We learn early in our careers that what we measure is what gets improved. If you are serious about growing a profitable business that is cash flow positive, then chart your critical success factors. Have a chart for sales, profit, # of clients, average sales price, units produced, cost of goods or services... whatever you know is critical for your success.

Charts are great... everybody can read charts. It's obvious when you are ahead of goal or not!

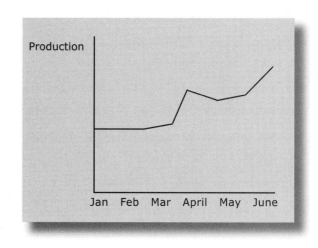

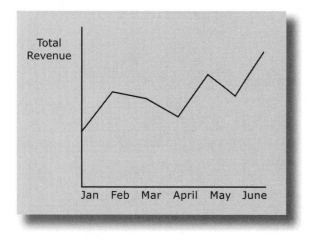

The key to setting meaningful Objectives is to identify goals that are:

- critical to your success and
- can be easily tracked
  (*Easily tracked = data is readily available and the specific target can be counted*)

Stated very simply, if you can not count or graph it over time (easily)... it's not an Objective.

On the Crafting Objectives exercise (page 64 - 69), we provide you with a number of frequently used Objectives... please note, all of them are graphable!

Microsoft Excel template for Scorecarding is on CD.

What does your Company Need More of Over Time? Less of?

Smart Objectives are Graphable Business Results! Use these graphs to brainstorm what your business needs MORE and LESS of over time in order to move to the next level of success. It is likely these are the things you will want to write Objectives for!

What does your Company need MORE of over time?

Examples:

- Sales
- Profit
- Higher Margins
- New Customers
- Repeat Customers
- Dollars/Sale
- Sales/Employee
- Production Yields
- Happy Employees

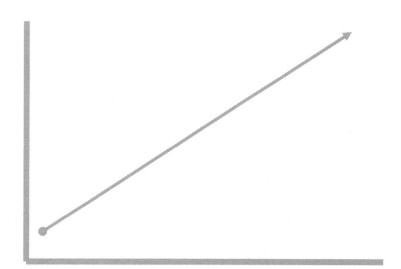

What does your Company need LESS of over time?

Examples:

- Lost sales
- Product Complaints
- Inactive customers
- Unhappy clients
- Downtime
- Excess Inventory
- Debt
- Employee turnover
- Missed Opportunities

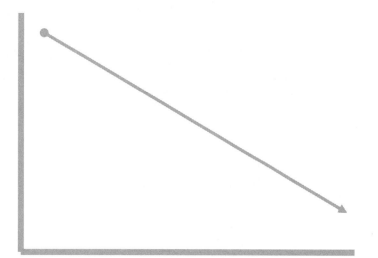

EXERCISE

We think starting with a blank piece of paper is a silly idea. There is no great mystery to writing a solid set of Objectives for your company... in fact, there is actually a formula or pattern. The four categories of Objectives and the fill-in-the-blank templates below are designed to help you think about your business from a holistic perspective... and to teach you how to write simple, clear and precise Objectives.

Financial

Total Sales or Revenues
Achieve total sales/revenues of $ _____ by 201____.

Gross Profit
Increase gross profit margin from _____ % to _____ % by _____.

Operating Expenses
Limit (reduce) monthly operating expenses to $ _____ ; or _____ % of sales.

Cash/Credit Cards/Credit Line/Debt
Build (maintain) cash reserves of $ _____; Limit credit card/debt to max of $ _____.

Owner Compensation
Increase owner's monthly salary from $ _____ to $ _____ by _____.

Profit before Tax
Increase profit before tax from $ _____ in 201____ to $ _____ in 201____.

Customer

New or Active Clients
Increase number of new/active clients from _____ to _____ by _____.

Units Sold (products, projects, programs, billable hours)
Increase number of _____ sold from _____ to _____ by _____.

Average Revenue per Sale
Increase average revenue per sale/client/project from $ _____ to $ _____.

Inquiries/Initial Trials
Increase # of _____ per month from _____ to _____ by _____.

First Purchases/Repeat Purchases
Increase # of _____ per month from _____ to _____ by _____.

Customer Service
Increase (decrease) _____ from _____ to _____ by _____.

Startups & Small Businesses

Step 1: Review Objectives templates and mark those that seem appropriate for your business.
Step 2: Open your OPBP Word doc.
Step 3: Craft up to nine Objectives using fill-in-the-blank templates selected below.
Note: Not all of these templates will be appropriate for your business... nor is this an exhaustive list.
See pages 66 – 69 for more sample templates.

Process Improvement

Marketing (web hits, public speaking, articles)
Increase # of _____ per month from _____ to _____ by _____.

Sales (appointments, proposals, close rate)
Increase # of _____ per week from _____ to _____ by _____.

Manufacturing (yields, waste, quality, cost, safety)
Increase (decrease) _____ from _____ to _____ by _____.

Operations/Services (quality, accuracy, timeliness, cost)
Increase (decrease) _____ from _____ to _____ by _____.

Finance/Accounting (invoicing, a/r collections, payable)
Increase (decrease) _____ from _____ to _____ by _____.

HR (new hires, training hours, overtime, # of employees)
Increase (decrease) _____ from _____ to _____ by _____.

Learning & Growth

Output per Employee (sales, units produced, people served)
Increase _____ per employee from _____ to _____ by _____.

Waste/Inefficiencies/Losses (time, materials, lost opportunities)
Decrease _____ waste/loss per month from _____ to _____ by _____.

Resource Utilization (equipment, facilities, technology)
Increase _____ productivity/utilization from _____ to _____ by _____.

Skills, Capabilities & Capacity
Increase _____ skills/capability/capacity from _____ to _____ by _____.

Achievement (promotions, awards, recognition)
Increase _____ from _____ to _____ by _____.

Owners, executives and managers tell us these templates help them craft clear and precise Objectives. Templates are meant to be models, not necessarily the precise wording or unit of measure. Some Objectives will use dollars, percents, units, days outstanding, etc.

Financial

Revenue/Sales: Total Company, Division, Department, Product Line, Program
Increase _____ sales from $_____ to $_____ in (month/qtr, year).

Profitability: Gross Margin, Operating Profit or Pre-tax Profit
Increase _____ profits from $_____ to $_____ (or % of sales).

Expenses: Cost of Goods/Services Sold, Operating Expenses, Bad Debt
Reduce _____ expense from $_____ to $_____ by _____ (date) (or % of sales).

Assets: Inventory, Accounts Receivables
Increase/decrease/maintain _____ levels from $_____ to $_____ by _____ (date).

Liabilities: Credit Line, Accounts Payable, Debt
Reduce _____ levels from $_____ to $_____ by _____ (date).

Customer

Number of Customers/Clients: New, Active, 1st Time Purchases
Increase number of _____ from _____ to _____ by _____.

Units Sold: Products, Cases, Billable Hours, Projects
Increase number of _____ sold from _____ to _____ by _____.

Average Sale: Dollars, Units, Profit
Increase average _____ from $_____ to $_____.

Frequency: Repeat Purchases, Referral Rate, Client Retention
Increase _____ from _____ to _____ by _____.

Quality: Customer Service, Complaints, Warranty Rate, Fulfillment Time
Increase (decrease) _____ from _____ to _____ by _____.

Businesses with Departments

Balanced Scorecard categories are designed to help you think about your business holistically and clearly define outcomes/results which are critical to your success. Note: Not all departments will have Objectives from all four categories... or need 9 Objectives.

Process Improvement

Marketing & Sales: Frequency/Effectiveness of Outreach, Responses, Success Rates
Increase (decrease) _____ from _____ to _____ by _____.

Manufacturing & Operations: Cycle Time, Yields, Waste, Quality
Increase (decrease) _____ from _____ to _____ by _____.

Finance, HR, Legal: Process Time, Quality, Effectiveness, Cost
Increase(decrease) _____ from _____ to _____ by _____.

Management & Decision Making: Process Time, Success/Failure Rates
Increase(decrease) _____ from _____ to _____ by _____.

Technology/Innovation: Time to Complete, Cost, Return on Investment
Increase(decrease) _____ from _____ to _____ by _____.

Learning & Growth

Output per Employee:
Increase _____ per employee from _____ to _____ ($, %, numerical value).

Resource Utilization: Equipment, Facilities, Technology
Increase _____ productivity/utilization from _____ to _____ by _____.

Waste/Inefficiencies/Losses: Time, Materials, Opportunities
Decrease _____ waste/loss per month from _____ to _____ by _____.

Skills, Capabilities & Capacity:
Increase _____ skills/capability/capacity from _____ to _____ by _____.

Achievement: Promotions, Awards, Recognition
Increase _____ from _____ to _____ by _____.

More Objectives...

On these two pages are another set of templates designed around the core business development processes of Marketing and Sales. These lists are more expansive and provide more choices for your consideration as you are developing your plan. Reminder: Your One Page Plan has the capacity for a total of nine Objectives. We also include some Personal/Well-Being Objectives for consideration.

Marketing

Contacts
Increase # of contacts per day from _____ to _____ by _____.

Appointments
Increase # of appointments per day from _____ to _____.

Presentations
Increase # of presentations per week from _____ to _____.

Closes
Increase # of closes per week from _____ to _____.

New Clients
Increase # of ideal clients from _____ to _____.

Public Speaking
Give at least _____ presentations in 1st half of 201____; _____ in 2nd half.

Publishing/Articles
Commit to writing _____ articles per quarter in 201____.

Special Events
Increase # of special events from _____ to _____ by _____.

Seminars/Educational Events
Increase # of seminars/workshops from _____ to _____ by _____.

Tradeshows/Conventions
Generate _____ prospects by attending _____ tradeshows/conventions in 201____.

Direct Mail Programs
Increase # of direct mail programs from _____ to _____ by _____.

COI - Center of Influence
Increase # of active COI's from _____ to _____. Meet with _____ COI's per month.

Sales, Marketing and Personal

Sales

Sales/Revenue per Month
Increase sales/revenue from $ _____ to $ _____ by _____.

Product Sales
Increase _____ product sales from $ _____ to $ _____ (or units).

Project/Program Sales
Sell _____ projects or programs at $ _____ for a total of $ _____.

Professional Service Sales
Sell _____ engagements at $ _____ for a total of $ _____.

Average Sale: Dollars, Units, Profit
Increase average _____ from $_____ to $_____.

Revenue per Client
Increase revenue per client from $ _____ to $ _____ by _____.

Average Engagement/Billable Hours
Increase average engagement from $ _____ to $ _____ by _____ (or hours).

Personal/Well-Being

Exercise
Increase exercise sessions per week from _____ to _____.

Weight
Decrease my weight from _____ to _____ by _____.

Vacation/Free Time
Commit to _____ weeks of vacation this year; _____ days of free time.

Community Service
Increase (decrease) total hours of community service from _____ to _____.

Personal Net Worth
Increase personal net worth from $ _____ to $ _____ by _____.

Sample Objectives

Here are six sets of Objectives from six very different companies. In these examples there are 6 to 8 Objectives that describe "what these companies will measure each month over the next 12 months to determine if they are on track." Some of these Objectives are rather traditional, others are a little unique. We hope they will get you to think creatively about your business... and what counts.

Amy Faust Wearable Art

- Grow sales to $150,000 in 2009 and $200,000 in 2010.
- Increase profitability to 50% of sales by July 31.
- Introduce 12 new jewelry products by January 31, 2009.
- Reduce direct costs by 40% through outsourcing manufacturing.
- Secure 2-3 catalog contracts with minimum orders of $25,000 by Sept 30.
- Register & attend 6-8 high end retail shows yearly & 2-3 wholesale shows.
- Reduce turnaround time for orders under $5000 to 3 wks. & large orders to 4-6 wks.
- Commit to 8 wks off per year and weekends when shows are not scheduled.

The Emergency IT Doctors

- Achieve 2010 sales of $500,000.
- Earn pre-tax profit of $60,000 after paying expenses and 3 principal salaries of $100,000.
- Increase number of active clients from 100 to 150 by June 30th.
- Reduce average client downtime from 6 hours to 4 hours.
- Reduce crisis response time from 2 hours to 1 hour.
- Increase percent of clients on remote technical service support program from 38% to 65%.
- Secure 150 PC audits in first six months of year to assure 33% conversion ratio.
- Reduce average OT from 26% to 10% by supplementing permanent staff w/ qualified temps.

Colorado Garden Window Company

- Achieve 2010 sales of $17 million.
- Earn pre-tax profits in 2010 of $1.5 million.
- Target Cost of Goods Sold at 38% of sales.
- Reduce inventory levels to 3.3 months on hand by August 31.
- Grow Garden Window Division at 8% per year & achieve $5.3M this year.
- Expand skylight/custom window product lines; grow sales to $7.5 million this year.
- Implement profit improvement programs & reduce product costs to 38%.
- Achieve 98% on time delivery with 98% order accuracy by 1st quarter.

There are several things to observe in these samples. Not all of the Objectives are financial, not all of them have dollars; however, all of these were first drafted using the fill-in-the-blank templates... and then edited. Also notice, all of these Objectives fit on a single line and there is only one "business result" per Objective.

Fresno Film Studio

- Raise initial $250,000 capital to build a sound stage film studio by Sept. 2010.
- Generate $150,000 on-going operating budget for student film productions annually.
- Recruit 100 liberal arts students into 4-year film study program by Sept. 2011.
- Evaluate program goals with student pre-eval (Sept) and post-eval (June) annually.
- Achieve 100% participation of film students in annual Slick Rock film festival.
- Place 70% of students into summer film workshops at SF Academy of Arts.

The Financial Designers

- Increase estate planning service fees from $725,000 to $900,000 in FY2008.
- Acquire an additional 75 target clients with average estate of $2 million.
- Acquire 12 new clients with minimum net worth of at least $5 million each.
- Achieve 98% retention of recurring maintenance fees w/ existing clients.
- Create minimum of one media exposure per month, per community. Total exposures 150.
- Increase average fee per plan from $8,500 to $10,000.
- Increase total earnings per partner after expenses from $135,000 to $160,000.

Alzheimer's Care Clinic

- Provide services to 350 individuals who have Alzheimer's or a related dementia.
- Provide case management services to 180 individuals in Tri-County area.
- Provide Ombudsman services in Tri-County; 4,800 contacts with residents.
- Operate the Tri-County Adult Day Support Center at 35 average daily census.
- Operate the Metro Adult Day Support Center at 26 average daily census.
- Serve 110,000 meals through the Meals on Wheels Program.
- Increase fee-for-service revenue to $525,000; 25% above last year.
- Obtain additional $125,000 in Foundation funding.

The Objectives... as Tamara Sees It

Setting objectives and measuring results are critical to your business success. The question to ask yourself is, "What results are important to me, my family, team members, or employees?" When you can answer this question, you have done something very important for your business...you have created a focus. You and everyone involved in your business know what is important.

Identifying what to measure can be difficult. In the beginning you will want to measure sales, number of new clients, expenses and profitability, whereas later your priorities may focus on streamlining production, inventory, delivery, and media exposure. As your business evolves, there will be new things you will choose to measure because they now have become much more important to you. Regardless of what you measure, your objectives will become your reliable friend as they help keep you focused and on track.

In my business I have objectives for sales/revenue and profit, but I also have objectives for membership growth, website traffic, and sponsorship revenues. These are particularly important to me because they will enable me to gauge progress towards both accomplishing my mission for my online community as well as my company vision. One of the more important objectives for the product brand side of my business is to increase the number of products we take to market. For example: "Launch 20 new Mom Invented® products by December 2011." This is an important objective because it supports my mission of celebrating the creativity of moms by launching innovative Mom Invented® products around the world; additionally new products fuel our revenue growth.

Another step in the process is to try to break your objectives down in a way that is most useful to you. For example, one objective may be to generate $120,000 in sales in the next 12 months. This can be broken down by month or quarter. However, it can also be broken down by the number of "clients" or by "projects." In other words, how much is each client worth? If the answer is $10,000, you know you need 10 clients to earn your desired sales of $120,000. If helpful, break this down even further by determining how many new clients you seek to gain each quarter or even each month.

Monitoring and tracking results over time are also critical and a very gratifying experience. They help you and your team literally "see" the results. When you can "see" the results, you can see what is working and what isn't and quickly make adjustments to unblock your progress.

If you are an experienced executive or owner, setting specific, measurable objectives and tracking them may be second nature for you. However, many first time – and repeat – entrepreneurs and business owners frequently avoid this process entirely. The drive to just build the business without setting objectives often prevails over the discipline of having people focus on achieving specific results. This is a major mistake because you are never able to build your team's understanding as to what you are working towards. Further, you also deprive yourself of the satisfaction of achieving the goals you declared were important to your success!

Sage Advice on Objectives

Get comfortable with your critical numbers

During a One Page Business Plan workshop I learned one of the "critical numbers" for my gourmet food business is gross profit… but I did not know what gross profit was; never heard of it. My husband and I found the formula on the web; we instantly understood it, and calculated it for our products. We determined our products have a gross margin between 45 - 55%; industry target is 42%. I highly encourage other women entrepreneurs to get comfortable with your "critical numbers." It will give you peace of mind!

Clarine Hardesty, President
Clarine's Florentines
www.clarinesflorentines.com

Learn how to read your financial statements; families are counting on it!

One day I woke up after 10 years of growing my national jewelry manufacturing and distribution business to over $2 million and realized I had amazingly learned how to read financial statements and do the analysis I needed to run my business… but that was not enough! Why? My business employed a diverse immigrant population…and supported their families. If I failed to have solid control of my cash flow, expenditures, receivables…100's of people would be seriously impacted. I rented a chief financial officer and got the additional help and tools I needed. My advice: Don't be afraid of accounting; it's glorified elementary school work. Learn it! Get the help you need to learn how to be in control of your company's finances. It is readily available. Remember, your employees and families are counting on you!

Tracy Holzman
President, Time Honored Patterns
President, Wild Bryde Jewelery 1993 - 2003

Create multiple streams of income!

Come up with a strategy that balances short-term and long-term revenue streams. Creating a variety of products that each supply a steady flow of income can keep your business progressing while you develop the next big thing. This approach can be invaluable in growing a self-sustaining, self-funded business.

Heather Bailey, Playful & Inventive Designer of All Things Happy
Heather Bailey Store
www.heatherbaileystore.com

Sage Advice on Objectives

Without specific goals, your team does not know what is important

I learned when people do not know what they are accountable for, they run from here to there. They work on the wrong things, their energy is scattered. Without specific goals from you, they do not know what is important. In the absence of goals, they will make up their own and they will likely be lower than yours. Everyone will be disappointed, and you may have put your business at risk. The solution: identify the top three things (must be measurable) you need to do to move your business forward. Clearly articulate these goals to your team, why they are important, create a blueprint for getting them done, assign responsibilities, monitor the implementation, measure the results frequently... celebrate the successes. If there are people that cannot produce, they are in the wrong job, maybe the wrong company.

Pat Poyle (former Advertising Director, Saturn Division, General Motors)
President, Henry Business Solutions
www.henrysolutions.net

Extreme approach to goal setting rarely works

As a female executive, I have often pondered the apparent "difference" between the male and female business brain and whether this is based on cultural, biological or neurological factors. In the area of setting objectives, I have observed that very often the male brain appears to be more focused on achieving the goal regardless of the obstacles in the way, whereas the female brain is often more attentive to navigating the obstacles in a way that avoids collateral damage. The extreme of both approaches has its pitfalls: a singular focus on results may leave a "swath of destruction" in its path, whereas dealing with obstacles one by one may lead to distraction and getting off course. One extreme can lead to apathy on the part of team members and the other can lead to confusion. Obviously, integrating the two approaches when setting objectives gets everyone on the "same page." That is why a business tool like the One Page Business Plan is an invaluable aid to any leader/executive who wants to set strong objectives while being mindful of the process needed to build alignment and commitment among team members. It works for both the female and male business brain!

Gail Patton DaMert, Ph.D.
Director, Neuromarketing Research, SalesBrain
CEO, DaMert Company 1990-2002

Non profits need to operate more like for-profit businesses.

Too often NGOs put off business planning due to staff capacity and difficulty in identifying measurable objectives. The One Page Business Plan more clearly links objectives to mission with a method that is straightforward, takes less staff time and gets people working on the right things! As women, we spend time helping others plan out their lives, and in the process, often give ourselves short shrift. *The One Page Business Plan for Women in Business,* invites us to ask ourselves the right questions, take a hard look at what we want, learn about ourselves and find out what is true for us now and going forward and then create a plan that makes it happen!

Lyn Ciocca McCaleb
Board Chair, The Coral Reef Alliance

Next Steps for Your Objectives

1 **REVIEW:** Do your Objectives answer these questions?

OBJECTIVE QUESTIONS:	YES/NO
Define the most critical business results you must achieve to be successful?	
Is each Objective graphable?	
Are these Objectives realistic? Achievable?	
Keep you, your team & resources focused on the most important outcomes & results?	
Do you have the date, systems & commitment to track these Objectives?	
Establish framework for accountability & incentive pay/bonus programs?	
Is each Objective owned by someone? Have a specific achievement date?	

2 **REFLECT:** Assuming the reader knows nothing about your business, do your Objectives clearly answer the question: *What are the critical business results we must achieve to be successful?*

3 **SHARE:** After reflecting on your Objectives for a few days, consider sharing them with at least a couple of people and asking them for feedback.

4 **COMPLETION!:** Satisfied with your Objectives? Go to the CD at the back of the book, find The One Page Business Plan template in the Forms and Templates folder, and type your Objectives into the template.

VISION
MISSION
OBJECTIVES
STRATEGIES
ACTION PLANS

Strategies

How will this business be built?

"Strategies define what will make your business successful over time!

It is your recipe for success!"

Success is rarely an accident. It is usually the result of executing a carefully crafted set of strategies. Strategies provide a blueprint or road map for building and managing a professional practice or a company. They also provide a comprehensive overview of the company's business model and frequently say as much about what the company will not do, as what it will do.

Strategies set the direction, philosophy, values, and methodology for building and managing your company. They establish guidelines and boundaries for evaluating business decisions. Following a predefined set of strategies is critical to keeping your professional practice on track.

One way of understanding strategies is to think of them as industry practices. Each industry has its leaders, its followers and its rebels; each has their own approach for capturing market share. Pay attention to the successful businesses in your industry and you can learn important lessons. You can also learn a lot from the failures.

Strategies are not secret. In fact, they are common knowledge and openly shared in every industry. Pick up any industry's publications and you will know precisely what the industry's leaders have to say about the opportunities and how to capitalize on them. These leaders will also share their current problems and their solutions. This is critical information for building and managing your business. Capture the best thinking/best practices from your industry leaders along with your creative ideas that will make your company unique and you will have a powerful set of strategies that drive you and your company forward!

In summary, Strategies are broad statements, covering multiple years that:

- Set the direction, philosophy, values
- Describe ideal clients, and how you will attract them
- Define your products, services and business model
- Establish guidelines for evaluating important decisions
- Set limits on what your company will do or will not do

A Simple Formula for Writing Strategies...

Business-building activity or goal
+
How it will be done

Here are a number of well-crafted Strategies using this simple formula:

Business Building Activity or Goal	How the goal will be accomplished
Become nationally known	thru public speaking, articles & media relations.
Attract young families	thru seminars, workshops & referrals.
Promote initial trial	thru in-store/restaurant tastings, coupons & advertising.
Generate repeat sales	w/ loyalty programs, monthly specials & limited promotional items.
Expand client base	by co-marketing w/ CPA's, attorneys & financial advisors.
Use special events	to attract new customers & cross/up sell to existing clients.
Use Internet	for awareness, credibility, building email list.
Attract & retain key employees	by being industry leader & known as fun place to work.
Minimize personal time on admin	thru use of virtual assistant & smart technology.
Exit business in 10 years	by selling to partners, merging w/ national firm or strategic partner.

Many people get confused about the difference between Objectives, Strategies and Action Plans. Over the next few pages we are going to help you understand the difference and make it very easy for you to craft a set of Strategies that answer these two critical questions:

- How will you build this business?
- What will make this business successful over time?

If you get confused, come back to this page and review the Simple Formula for Strategies and these examples.

What will make this business successful over time?

There are many moving parts to a successful business. There are a lot of decisions to be made. Many of the decisions are personal preference.

Keep in mind that nobody gets all the parts and pieces in place before they start. It takes time, probably three to five years. Review this list; use it as a catalyst to think about what will actually be necessary to make your business successful over time. As you are crafting your Strategies on pages 84 and 85, refer to this page.

- ☐ Personal expertise, energy & passion
- ☐ Previous business success
- ☐ Marketing, sales & technical knowledge
- ☐ Compelling product or service
- ☐ Clear & compelling value proposition
- ☐ Understand current market conditions
- ☐ Ability to self-fund or raise capital
- ☐ Solid reputation in industry/community
- ☐ Ability to form strategic alliances
- ☐ Compelling brand
- ☐ Strong product name(s)
- ☐ Clear pricing policy
- ☐ Trademarks/Patents
- ☐ Effective sales & marketing systems
- ☐ Customer service support systems
- ☐ Professional website
- ☐ Reliable source for products/services

- ☐ Quality control systems
- ☐ Financial/Accounting controls & systems
- ☐ Business plan & budget
- ☐ Legal & HR advisors
- ☐ Business office
- ☐ Computers, software & support
- ☐ Administrative support
- ☐ Insurance coverage
- ☐ Health, benefit, retirement programs
- ☐ Licensing & franchising
- ☐ Public speaking & publishing
- ☐ Employees or Subcontractors
- ☐ Personal mentor/coach/advisor
- ☐ Family Support
- ☐ Peace of Mind
- ☐ Free time

Researching Strategies Appropriate for Your Business:

Finding appropriate strategies for your business is not difficult. Information is readily available to you for free or at minimal cost.

There are multiple professional, industry, trade and community associations that serve your niche. Ask other people in your line of business where they go to learn the latest trends in your industry. Go online and explore.

Be careful! The amount of information can be overwhelming. The key question is: Which strategies will you select that will be appropriate for your business? Listen to your intuition and check out what you learn with other business professionals you trust. Then craft them as Strategies and put them into your plan.

 **interview**
EXERCISE

Where Does Success Come From?

Where does success come from? What will it look like in the future? Think about your past experiences and what you have learned from them. Have a friend, associate or advisor ask you these questions and record your responses.

Where have you been successful in the past? Where has your business been successful in the past?	How can you expand upon these successes?
What were your past mistakes? Mistakes your company or organization has made?	What have you learned from these mistakes?
What ideas have you not acted on?	Which of these ideas will you go forward with?

Opportunities & Threats

Review the last three issues of your industry's trade, professional or association journals and answer the questions below.

What and where are the opportunities?	How can you capitalize on them?
What threats exist?	**How can you minimize the threats and/or turn them into opportunities?**

Strategies for 2010 and Beyond

Opportunities & Trends

- Specialized products for women, Baby Boomers, ethnic groups and over 70 crowd.

- Sell your products anywhere in world w/ the web (theoretically).

- Market still loves highly creative, new products. Most still come from small businesses.

- Giant opportunities in all things green and health care.

Threats & Warnings

- Consumers are even more price conscious. Manufacturing in US will be difficult.

- Low prices do not translate to low quality. Commit to excellence.

- Someone else is doing what you are doing... do it better, faster, cheaper.

- Personal selling still trumps technology... pick up the phone.

Bend the Curve
Prioritizing your Strategies

Bend the Curve is one of the most powerful business tools in this book! And it is very visual. With just a little bit of explanation, everybody instantly understands it. This tool graphically demonstrates the critical relationship between an Objective and its supporting Strategies and Action Plan.

Here's the basic concept. Objectives are graphable business results as we learned in Chapter 5. Almost everyone wants their sales and profit graphs to go up overtime...and their costs, quality issues and lost sales charts to go down overtime. The question is, "what you can you do to significantly bend these curves either up or down...overtime?" The answer...Strategies! How do you implement Strategies? The answer...business-building projects or programs defined in your Action Plans.

You can use Bend the Curve to brainstorm how you will "bend" any of your Objectives and/or you can use this process to prioritize all the wild and crazy ways generated in your brainstorming down to 3 – 5 Strategies you are going to act on. Then you will define the key projects and programs that implement the Strategies.

Here is an example of Bend the Curve for sales growth:

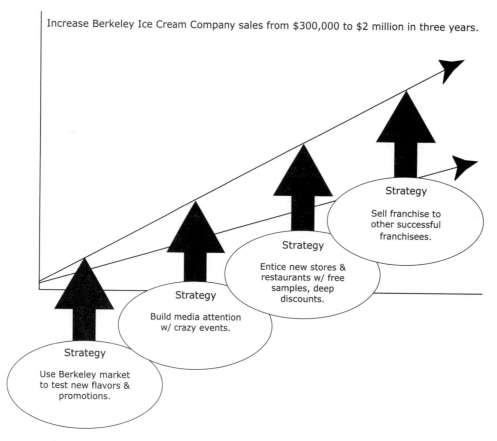

Increase Berkeley Ice Cream Company sales from $300,000 to $2 million in three years.

Strategy — Use Berkeley market to test new flavors & promotions.

Strategy — Build media attention w/ crazy events.

Strategy — Entice new stores & restaurants w/ free samples, deep discounts.

Strategy — Sell franchise to other successful franchisees.

Action Plans

- 4 new flavors per year
- Monthly wild events
- 8 seasonal promos

- Hire PR firm
- Partner w/ unemployed actors
- Create videos for TV & Internet

- Develop list of gourmet markets/rest
- Create limited promos you can't say no to
- Video happy customers

- Hire franchise experts to manage process
- Promote opportunity at national franchise conventions

Step 1: Draft a significant growth Objective for the next 2, 3 or 5 years.
Step 2: Brainstorm up to four Strategies that are necessary to achieve the Objective in Step 1.
Step 3: Identify 2 to 4 key Action Plans per Strategy. Action Plans are typically Projects or Programs.

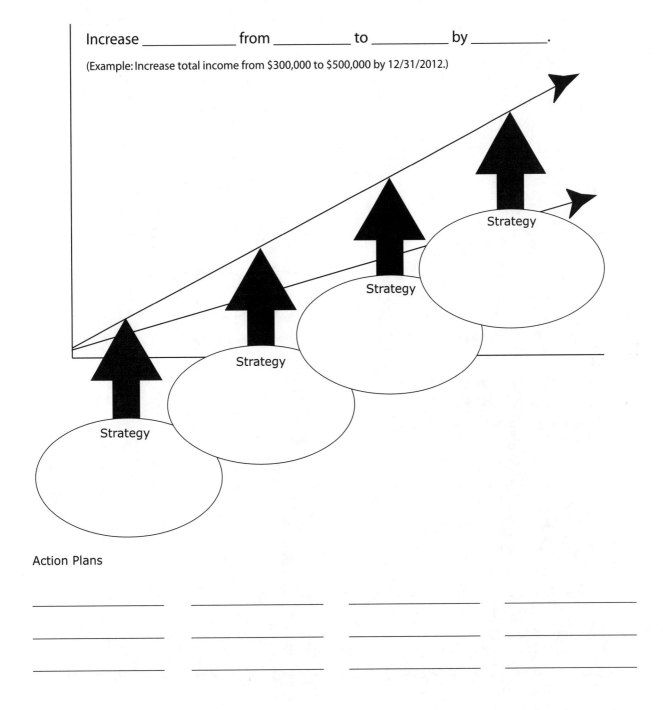

Increase _____ from _____ to _____ by _____.

(Example: Increase total income from $300,000 to $500,000 by 12/31/2012.)

Action Plans

_____   _____   _____   _____

_____   _____   _____   _____

_____   _____   _____   _____

Crafting Your Strategies

Strategies define how you will build your business and what will make it successful over time. Entrepreneurs, owners and executives tell us these templates help them think about their business from a holistic perspective... and teach them how to write simple, but very powerful Strategies. Templates are meant to be examples and learning aids, not necessarily the precise wording.

Customer

Positioning
Become locally/nationally/internationally known for _____.

Opportunities
Focus on _____, _____ & _____ trends/opportunities.

Awareness & Initial Trial
Create awareness & initial trial by _____, _____ & _____.

Repeat Purchase
Encourage repeat purchases by _____, _____ & _____.

Promotions & Discounts
Offer _____ & _____ promotions/discounts to encourage _____.

Customer Service
Provide excellent service by _____, _____ & _____.

Process Improvement

Planning, Execution & Accountability
Strengthen _____ & _____ processes by _____ & _____.

Sales & Marketing
Improve _____ & _____ processes by _____, _____, _____.

Customers
Improve _____ & _____ customer processes by _____ & _____.

Employees
Enhance _____, _____ & _____ employee processes by _____.

Service Providers, Supply Chain, Manufacturing
Streamline _____, _____ & _____ vendor processes by _____.

Quality & Safety
Improve/expand _____, _____ quality processes by _____, _____.

Step 1: Review list of Strategies.
Step 2: Place a check mark next to those that seem appropriate for your business.
Step 3: Open your OPBP Word doc.
Step 4: Craft up to nine Strategies using templates to get started, then edit as necessary.

Learning & Growth

Industry Knowledge/Best Practices
Expand/improve _____ & _____ best practices by _____ & _____.

Communication & Presentation Skills
Improve communication/presentation skills by _____, _____ & _____.

Technology
Invest in/learn _____ & _____ technologies to improve _____ & _____.

Financial Literacy
Increase company's financial literacy by _____, _____ & _____.

Professional Development
Develop/improve _____ & _____ skills through _____ & _____ programs.

Personal Productivity
Improve personal productivity _____, _____ & _____.

Financial

Rate of Growth
Grow business at _____ % per year by _____, _____ & _____.

Profitability
Assure profitability by _____, _____ & _____.

Expense Control
Control expenses by _____, _____ & _____.

Financing
Finance business by _____, _____ & _____.

Profit Improvement
Continuously improve profitability by _____, _____ & _____.

Capital Projects
Invest in _____, _____ & _____ to support _____ & _____.

Sample Strategies

Here are six sets of strategies, from six very different companies. In these examples there are 6 to 8 strategies that describe the "essence of what will make these companies successful over time."

The HR Consulting Group

- Become known for preventing catastrophic employee problems that destroy businesses.
- Attract clients with 50 to 500 employees, business owners who want preventive solutions.
- Promote initial trial through our monthly employer council meetings & low-cost guide books.
- Generate revenues thru preventive audits & assessments, training programs & consulting.
- Use technology/Internet for tele-classes, audits & assessments, & selling training guides.
- Strategically align our firm w/ local employment law attorneys, CPAs & business consultants.
- Continue to create books, guides, audiotapes, & assessment products from existing services.
- Build a business that is ultimately not dependent on my presence; which will make it sellable.

Oklahoma Jazz Hall of Fame

- Increase revenues and surplus by promoting performances, galas & space rental.
- Build/attract membership base by promotion, advertising & organization.
- Increase revenue by offering diverse programming, increasing event frequency & mktg.
- Build donations by dev a capital campaign plan, hiring a dev consultant and a grant writer.
- Engage and educate youth by use of library, computers & practices.
- Expand scholarship endowment by corporate & individual donations & grants.
- Improve Board eff. by targeted recruiting, pre-evaluation & involvement through planning.
- Attract/retain volunteer base by membership, marketing & external programs.

Clarine's Florentines

- Promote hand-made, gluten-free, European inspired, gourmet qual. thru creative pkg/PR/web.
- Increase # of high-end gourmet stores through personal marketing & referrals.
- Promote initial trial w/ in-store demos, free restaurant trials & individual serving packaging.
- Use Internet to sell products w/ online store, promote demo locations & share stories/recipes.
- Attract media attention w/creative stories; participate in nat'l trade shows for brand visibility.
- Creatively partner w/ other small gourmet food companies; create news w/ the Sweet Mafia.
- Lease commercial kitchen & sublet to other mfg'ers to improve quality & reduce expenses.
- Have fun! Stay balanced! Have plenty of time for my new family! Enjoy life!

These strategies describe business models, best practices, culture and personal preferences. All were initially created with the fill-in-the-blank templates and then edited. Note that each strategy fits on a single line.

Portland Insurance Agency

- Become locally known for excellence in "family & business insurance solutions".
- Build long term relationships w/ prominent bus. leaders - create consistent referral source.
- Maximize visibility by serving on community, non-profit, & prof boards. Motto: Give Back Often!
- Mine existing client base for "A" clients; use seminar marketing system to find "B"clients.
- Strategic Mktg Alliances - selectively align w/ CPAs, attorneys, auto dealers, real estate profs.
- Sell thru education; use computer presentations to assure consistent message delivery.
- Staffing - hire professionals, provide quality training, 1:1 mentoring, track perf, reward Winners.

Eye 2 Eye Graphics

- Attract women business owners w/ multiple products/services & are expanding their business.
- Core Products/Services are brand strategy, design, & on-going brand support.
- Re-evaluate client process by finalizing contracts, review questionnaires & project mgmt system.
- Encourage rpt purchases w/promo pieces, project follow-up processes & using design wish lists.
- Inc public knowledge by attending events, forming partnerships, publishing articles, & speaking.
- Tgt clients/partners by updating profile, creating Ideal Partner profile & updating svc packages.
- Incr profitability by monitoring expenses, charging for extras, & updating pricing strategy.
- Inc visibility by speaking, articles in trade papers/magazines, blogging & promote e-zine.

Sarah Oliver Handbags

- Target fashion conscious women through PR and marketing campaigns.
- Target and present to new high-end gift mkts.
- Participate in sales events that highlight and honor locally made goods.
- Encourage repeat purchases via new, innovative lines and brooch customization.
- Offer samples sales 2x annually to reduce inventory and push prior season product.
- Find cost effective vendors in the areas of washing, plastic fabrication, finishing.
- Consistently improve manufacturing processes to reduce labor, materials & overhead expenses.
- Hire senior citizens for knitting to keep production local

The Strategies... as Tamara Sees It

Strategies explain how you will build your business, in essence, your recipe for success. The question to ask yourself is, "What will make my business successful over time?"

To illustrate, here are three of my most important strategies I have used to build my business. You hopefully can see how they directly support my objectives and my mission:

Mission:

> "Celebrate the creativity of moms by launching innovative Mom Invented® products around the world."

Objective:

- Launch 20 new Mom Invented® products by December 2011.

Strategies:

- Conduct product searches through our online community.
- License products invented by moms and credit them for their creativity on the packaging.
- Partner with leading retailers who will commit to selling the new products.

Strategies are the stepping stones that lead to building your business and are a place where you can leverage your natural abilities as a woman. In the six years I have run my current business, as well as in other previous professional roles, I have been amazed by the creativity of women. Our advantage -- yes, ADVANTAGE -- is a lack of formal business background or training. I say and believe this because we are not constrained by how "things are done" in other business environments.

Nobody exhibits this better than Sarah Oliver, founder of Sarah Oliver Handbags. Knowing she had to have her bags knitted by hand to fit her vision, she chose to hire women living at senior homes to make her spectacular handbags. Not only has she created excitement and camaraderie among her knitters, but she has gained the benefit of their talent and added meaning to her brand with an extraordinary media hook. Brilliant strategy!

Strategies are where your instinctive creativity can and MUST come out to build a thriving business!

Sage Advice on Strategies

Start out right!

Take the time to set up your business properly. Incorporate, get your business and resale licenses, file your fictitious name statement, register trade names and trademarks, and apply for patents. Start out ready to grow so you don't have to stop your momentum to take care of the things that should have been in place from the beginning.

Heather Bailey, Playful & Inventive Designer of All Things Happy
Heather Bailey Store
www.heatherbaileystore.com

People are watching; Set highest standards of quality!

Our products are handmade by seamstresses in San Miguel de Allende; each an original work of art. The work of one seamstress, Dolores, was not up to par of the others, but I failed to call her on it. The other seamstresses observed my behavior. One day one of the women bravely spoke to me in private and shared that she and the other women were not proud of this woman's work. I attempted to correct the situation with Dolores, but was unsuccessful, and had to let her go. Amazingly the quality of all of the women's work significantly increased and my business exploded.

Patrice Wynne, Founder
San Miguel Designs (formerly founder/owner Gaia Bookstore)
www.sanmigueldesigns.com

Keep your focus narrow, you don't have the resources to be everything to everybody.

I started out thinking that targeting "women" would suffice. What I have learned is the world of women is much too vast. I needed to refine, over and over again, the small group of women who truly are a good fit for what I offer. This has optimized my marketing efforts because now that I know who they are I know where I am most likely to find them. There is a common fear, especially when starting a business, that if you narrow your focus you'll miss opportunity. The reality is if you don't narrow your focus, you're less likely to succeed because you don't have the resources needed to be everything to everybody.

Cynthia Riggs, President
Women Building Business
www.womenbuildingbusiness.com

Build your business as if you have no money!

Build your business as if you have no money. It will make you think in new, creative ways and keep you from overspending as you nurture your business through the growing pains into a mature business.

Jessica Siegel, Classical Harpist, President
Harps Etc.
www.harpsetc.com

Sage Advice on Strategies

Create buzz early!

It is really important to "get out there" well before you have your product on store shelves or launch your business. Create the buzz, talk to people in your field, and do lots of networking well in advance of your "debut". When you have a group of people that know you and your story, when the time comes to sell your product or open your business, these are the people that will have known you "way back when" and will be more than willing to help you succeed. In today's world it truly takes a village, and early on I created new friends in places like www.mominventors.com, www.mompreneursonline.com and www.startup-nation.com. I would not be where I am without their support, which they gave LONG before I launched my product.

Leslie Haywood, Mom Inventor, Founder & President
Charmed Life Products LLC
www.grillcharms.com

Pick suppliers as carefully as you select employees

I credit my business and its success on picking the right people and the incredible talent up front. The mistakes I made were in the people and suppliers that were not committed to my business; in fact, some were dishonest. So, do the due diligence up front to find out about everyone who touches your business, whether you are spending $500 on them or $50,000. Whether it's a lawyer, accountant, or even a PR manager, don't be afraid to ask for references and concrete success stories from other businesses like yours that they've dealt with. If they have a great reputation, they won't be afraid to share it and allow you to speak with their other customers and clients. If not, work with someone else. I learned that ultimately, the people you work with on a daily basis will make or break your business. In the end, it is not just your efforts, it's theirs as well.

Cathy Bennett, Founder
How Fast Time Flies™
www.howfasttimeflies.com

Learn to state your price without apologizing

Far too many women, including a former version of myself, don't value their products and services adequately. In fact, we have a tendency to under-price them. It was not until I saw my male colleagues getting 5 to 10 times the fee for the same work that I developed the courage to value myself and price my products and services at their full value. I began to handle my fear about being turned down at a higher price point by practicing in front of the mirror. Fake it 'till you make it works! Now when someone asks me what I charge, I take a deep breath, look them in the eye, state my price without apology and wait for a response. I encourage you to do the same. It works! People will pick up on your confidence and see that you value yourself and your work and will want to do business with you because of it.

Toni Nell, Founder
Springboard Consulting
www.springboardconsulting.biz

Next Steps for Your Strategies

1 **REVIEW:** Do your Strategies answer these questions?

STRATEGY QUESTIONS:	YES/NO
How you will build this business and what will make it successful over time?	
Describe ideal clients and how you will attract them?	
Define your products, services and business model?	
How you will Bend the Curve to achieve your key Objectives	
Define process improvements & key learnings critical to your long-term success?	
Define how your company will be financially successful over time?	
Set limits on what your company will do or will not do?	

2 **REFLECT:** Assuming the reader knows nothing about your business, do your Strategies clearly answer the question: *How will this business be built and what will make it successful over time?*

3 **SHARE:** After reflecting on your Strategies for a few days, consider sharing your Strategies with at least a couple of people and asking them for feedback.

4 **COMPLETION!:** Satisfied with your Strategies? Go to the CD at the back of the book, find The One Page Business Plan template in the Forms and Templates folder, and type your Strategies into the template.

VISION
MISSION
OBJECTIVES
STRATEGIES
ACTION PLANS

Action Plans

What is the work to be done?

> *"Business building projects always compete with daily fire fighting.*
>
> *Allocate time and resources to the projects that will build your business."*

Action Plans are business-building projects, programs and initiatives that implement your Strategies and define the critical initiatives necessary to achieve your Objectives. This is the work that must be done to build your business!

All entrepreneurs, executives and business owners struggle with the balance between "daily fire fighting" and "business-building" projects. The Action Plans you formulate should be significant business-building projects, not a list of your normal, ongoing tasks and routines. Your business plan is not your job description.

It is highly unlikely every Strategy and Objective will have an Action Plan in this plan! While this may seem counter intuitive, keep in mind your Vision, Mission and Strategies under normal circumstances reflect a multi-year perspective (3 – 5 years or more). If you are writing a three (3) year plan, the Objectives and Action Plans will reflect the three year planning horizon. If you are crafting a one year plan, the Objectives and Action Plans will focus on what you want to accomplish in the next twelve months.

If you find you have more than nine (9) Action Plans, it's possible you need to write a separate One Page Plan for one or more of the major projects... or more likely, you have defined too many projects for this year.

"Work" may be defined three ways:

- Major business building projects or programs
- Significant infrastructure projects
- Programs/Projects that bend the curves and/or trend lines

A Simple Formula for Writing Action Plans...

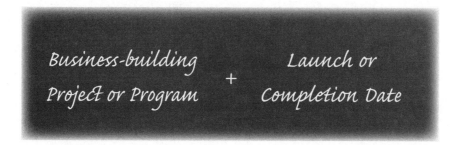

Business-building Project or Program + *Launch or Completion Date*

Here are some examples using the formula:

- Complete eight (8) ready-to-wear designs for trade show in Aspen by March 31st.
- Purchase and install 3 new computer aided knitting machines by July 31st.
- Introduce new packaging design & individually wrapped products by March 1st.
- Launch website w/ online store capabilities by Oct 10th.
- Complete installation of CRM system by Sept. 30th; New GL by Dec. 31st.
- Develop community speaking program (6/30). Deliver monthly talks Sept - Dec.
- Hire Project Manager by April 15th to secure grant funding & construction proposals.
- Complete lease negotiations, facility rehab & move in by Oct. 15th.

Work "Bends" the Curve... Project Prioritization

In the Strategy section we used the "Bend the Curve" visual to identify the major opportunities that have the potential to significantly grow your business over the next 3 to 5 years. We can again use this visual model to help identify and prioritize the major projects and programs you and your team are going to focus on in the next twelve months.

When you have agreed on the projects that will bend the curve, assign completion dates and responsibility... then craft the Action Plans. Each of these projects is a potential candidate for your One Page Business Plan! Also be sure to calculate the expense and capital budgets for these projects and get them into your One Page Budget Worksheet, which is included in the Women in Business Tool Kit CD.

Step 1: Craft an Objective (or use one already created) that is critical to this year's success.
Step 2: Brainstorm 2 - 4 projects, programs or actions that have potential to bend the curve.
Step 3: Identify the people, estimated expense & capital budgets required to implement projects.
Step 4: Craft appropriate Action Plan(s) with completion date(s) and personnel responsible.
Step 5: Input expense estimates and capital requirements into your budget.

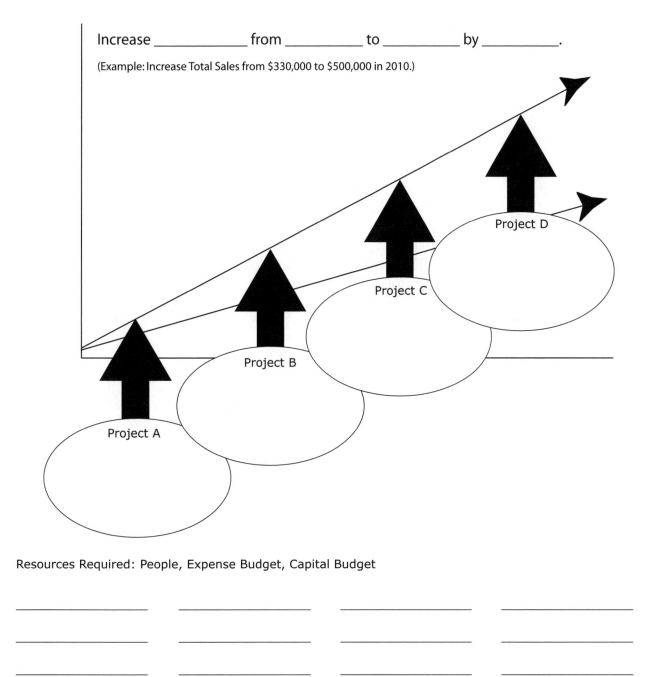

Increase _____ from _____ to _____ by _____.

(Example: Increase Total Sales from $330,000 to $500,000 in 2010.)

Project A

Project B

Project C

Project D

Resources Required: People, Expense Budget, Capital Budget

_____   _____   _____   _____

_____   _____   _____   _____

_____   _____   _____   _____

The One Page Planning Wheel

The One Page Planning Wheel is another visual tool that helps visualize key projects over the entire year.

Most people have little problem identifying critical tasks and near-term projects that need to be completed in the next six days... or six weeks. But the identification, prioritization and calendaring of significant projects and programs in the second half of the year... or beyond, can be difficult when the focus is so often on short term results.

Use The One Page Planning wheel as a tool to brainstorm which projects and programs you are going to start, and/or complete in the next twelve months... and when you will work on them. In the brainstorming phase, identify all major projects, then refine the list down to two or three projects per quarter.

Remember, your One Page Business Plan can accommodate up to nine Action Plans.

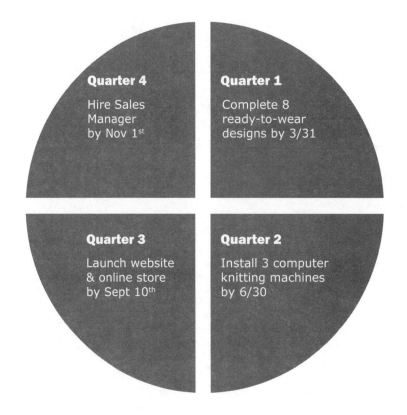

There are four quarters in a year. List one or two major business-building projects that must be accomplished in each of the next four quarters in order to implement your Strategies and achieve your Objectives. When complete, type your Action Plans into The One Page Business Plan template that is in the Women in Business Tool Kit CD.

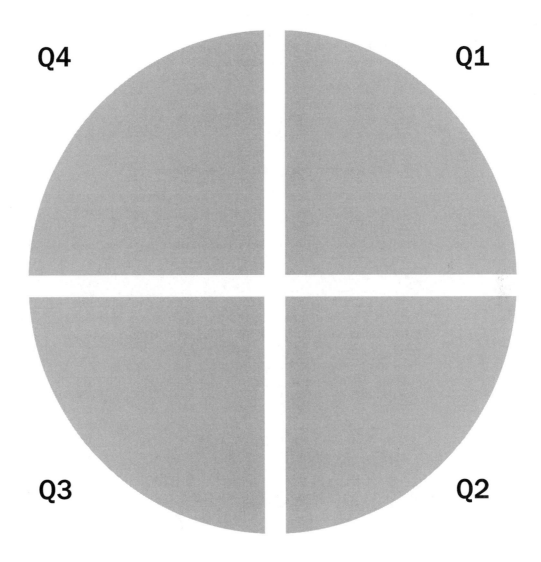

Remember: Time exists so that you do not have to do everything at once.

The Action Plans... as Tamara Sees It

Action Plans answer the question, "What is the work to be done to implement the strategies?" You can also think of Action Plans as business-building projects or programs.

Action is another place I personally think women have an advantage! We juggle non-stop. Whether you have children or not you most likely still maintain most of the relationships in your life (extended family and friends). And we have the ability to get what needs to be done... done!

There is one point of caution that I must raise with which I have personally wrestled. The potential for action is infinite but the available time, money and energy are not. The key is to prioritize and to focus on actions that have the greatest impact. The focus needs to be on activities that truly move the business forward in relation to available resources – in other words...YOU.

The challenge is distractibility because the "pulls" in every direction are large. A plan should not include more than nine Action Plans. But, as a business manager, you can probably think of a dozen "actions" you will take in one day-- before lunch! Most of those actions are urgent to-do's, not business building projects. It is highly unlikely you have more than nine significant business building projects you need to complete in any year.

So, go ahead and start out with all of the business building projects that come to mind. Then prune and prioritize the list down to those that have finite completion dates as well as those that specifically implement your strategies and have a significant impact on achieving your objectives. This does not mean that you will not do other things. It simply means that you are keenly focused on the priority projects that build your business.

If you are bringing a product to market or launching a new service, think about what actions you need to take with specific dates that will move things forward. If you miss a deadline, don't criticize yourself. Instead, create a new deadline and give yourself the gift of doing it on time. This will be rewarding and give you the courage to do the next thing on your list. For me, nothing is better than taking action because action builds a business!

Sage Advice on Action Plans

Frances Ford Coppola says "Get out of your head, try something!"

I was lucky to get directorial training from Frances Ford Coppola when I still worked in film. When actors wanted to endlessly discuss all of the possible interpretations of their roles to avoid getting on stage, Coppola would say, "Just try anything and I can then give you direction when I see what you bring to the table."

Women seem to feel they have to know everything before they do one thing. They tend to take classes and workshops to avoid getting their product (or service) to market to see if it will sell. I encourage women to take action to see what actually works and what doesn't. You can always hone your project, program or product once you get feedback!

Allison Bliss, President
Allison Bliss Consulting, a marketing & communications agency
www.allisonbliss.com

Between Regret and Failure, Failure seemed like the better option. Act on your ideas!

People have ideas all the time and never act on them! What was it that gave you the push to actually do what other people just think about doing? This is going to sound like a strange answer, but it was actually fear. The fear of the regret I would feel if two years down the road I saw MY product on the shelves by someone else because I didn't act was so much more powerful than my fear of failure that I didn't really have a choice. Between regret and failure, to me, failure (should that have been the case) seemed like a better option.

Leslie Haywood, Mom Inventor, Founder & President
Charmed Life Products LLC
www.grillcharms.com

Effective execution creates success!

I always heard "Business is business"... which led me to believe that the "human" aspect of business was less important. What I've learned along the way, is that being "human" is the cornerstone of building a successful business. Work with integrity. Treat people right, customers and employees. Do the right thing, even when no one is watching. These tenets, coupled with a strong plan and effective execution, will create your success!

Gwen Gallagher, President
Old Republic Home Protection
www.orhp.com

Sage Advice on Action Plans

Jump off the fast track to better balance babies and career.

The ideal life is doing something rewarding outside the home while feeling satisfied at home with the priorities you have made. This is difficult and you have to be creative and perseverant to make it happen. Start your own business. Ask your boss to let you work part-time or to try job-sharing. Ask to work from home once a week. Ask to work four days a week. Ask to cut your hours by 20%. Put a plan in place and present your case. Be ready to do it on a trial basis to prove that it will work. Find ways to be more productive – save time on the non-essentials/non-rewarding aspects of your life. Hire a house cleaner – I will sooner forgo eating out, the movies and wine, than my twice-a-month cleaners. Go on regular dates. Exercise – it saves time! I guarantee it – and you feel better.

Christine Tande, President
Tandehill Human Capital
www.tandehill.com

Manage your time by designing a model week

You don't get to the top of Mount Everest by wandering around and you won't have a successful business by wandering around. You need a good business plan and you need a solid model week. Manage your time by designing a model week that properly allocates time to essential marketing, sales and administrative activities. Engage your mental focus, emotional energy and time to execute on the activities that will make you successful. Your business is like a basketball game... some score points and some just dribble. Commitment to a strong business plan coupled with a clear model week will help you to score in life and in your career!

Diane Ruebling, President
The Ruebling Group LLC
Former Group VP American Express Financial Advisors
www.rueblingroup.com

Next Steps for Your Action Plans

1 **REVIEW:** Do your Action Plans answer these questions?

ACTION PLAN QUESTIONS:	YES/NO
Major business-building projects?	
Significant infrastructure projects?	
Programs/Projects that bend the curves and/or trend lines?	

2 **REFLECT:** Assuming the reader knows nothing about your business, do your Action Plans clearly define the specific actions necessary to implement Strategies and to achieve the Objectives?

3 **SHARE:** After reflecting on your Action Plans for a few days, consider sharing your Action Plans with at least a couple of people and asking them for feedback.

4 **COMPLETION!:** Satisfied with your Action Plans? Go to the CD at the back of the book, find The One Page Business Plan template in the Forms and Templates folder, and type your Action Plans into the template.

■ V I S I O N
■ M I S S I O N
■ OBJECTIVES
■ STRATEGIES
■ ACTION PLANS

Assembling and Polishing the Plan

*"Congratulations!
Your plan is now
in writing.*

*Step back, review
it with others.*

*Refine it until it
represents your
best thinking."*

Assemble Your Plan onto One Page!

Select one of The One Page Business Plan templates from the Women in Business Tool Kit CD and type in each of the five elements of the plan you created using the various exercises.

Step Back and Review Your Plan

How does it look to you? If you are like most people, some parts of your plan will be complete, while other parts will still need editing and additional detail. Don't rush the process! Make the obvious changes now, but allow some time to reflect on your plan.

Carry the plan with you; it's only one page! As new ideas and insights appear, capture them on paper. Review the Polishing and Edit suggestions on the next page. Most people find it takes about three drafts to get their plans in solid shape... don't cut the process short. Too much depends on it.

Review Your Plan with Others

You have a plan... now review it with your partners, team, and/or trusted advisors. Have them ask you clarifying questions. Take good notes on the feedback; you might consider recording the feedback sessions. Update your plan with the feedback you decide is appropriate.

Have Partners? Employees? Have them Create their Plan

Executives, managers and employees are expensive! After you have reviewed your plan with your team, and they have had a chance to ask clarifying questions, give them 3 to 7 business days to create their One Page Business Plan. Encourage them to work together; the plans will be more cohesive as a result. Have partners? Encourage them to create their plan, then meet to review and compare plans. Make appropriate changes to bring them into alignment.

Balance and Align the Plans

Balancing the plans is a process that ensures all of the functions within your company will be working together, on the right projects and programs, in the proper sequence, at the right time... and not at cross purposes.

When your organization's plans are balanced and aligned... you can have everyone, literally, working on the same page!

Editing and Polishing the Plan

Here is a list of ideas and tips to polish your plan:

Overall Review

- Does your Vision Statement describe what you are building?

- Will your Mission Statement attract new clients? Drive employee behavior? Is it memorable?

- Are your Objectives measurable, dated and graphable?

- Do your Strategies describe what will make your business successful over time?

- Are your Action Plans significant business-building projects? Will they achieve your Objectives?

Order and Abbreviation

- Edit Objectives, Strategies, and Action Plan statements to one line.

- Eliminate all unnecessary words and phrases.

- Abbreviate words when necessary.

- Use symbols like "&" in lieu of "and" to save space.

- Use "k" or "m" for thousands and "M" for millions.

- Communicate priority of Objectives, Strategies, and Action Plans by placing them in the proper order.

Creative Considerations

- Use bullets to make key points stand out.

- Highlight key phrases in italics.

Strengthening Exercises

- Edit Vision, Mission and Strategy until they are enduring statements that "resonate"!

- Drop low-priority items. Remember, "less can produce more."

- Refine Objectives and Action Plans to be specific, measurable, and define accountability.

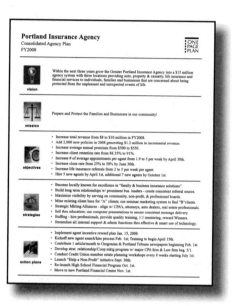

Involve Others

- Few people can write a solid plan by themselves; ask others for feedback.

- Ask your reviewers:
  - Is this plan really strategic? Too optimistic? Too pessimistic?
  - Does it include all of the critical initiatives I have been talking about?
  - Is it too risky? Too safe?
  - Does it reflect my best thinking?
  - What have I overlooked? What do you see that I missed?

- Listen to the feedback, take notes, and ask clarifying questions.

- Revise and update plan for feedback.

- Ask for another round of feedback.

- Most people find it takes at least three drafts to have a solid plan.

- Repeat until you and your reviewers agree it is solid.

Resources, Timelines and Budgets

Having a plan is critical to your success. Here are a few thoughts on other important processes that will help assure your success.

Define the Required Resources

Every project, program and initiative in your plan will need resources... or it will not happen. For each project identify the people, expenses, capital budget and any other resources required to fully execute the plan. The process of identifying the resources may cause you to realize you may not have the capability or capacity of implementing the plan you just wrote. If that is the case, go back and revise the plan.

Project Timelines

Review your project start and completion dates. Are they realistic? One of the major problems with all planning processes is the tendency to think we can do more than we actually can. When we complete a major project or initiative... we feel smart! When we have a list of projects that we have not started or are half done... we feel defeated. Take another hard look at your projects for this next year... would you be extraordinarily pleased if you completed just one or two of them? If so, adjust your plan.

Alignment with Partners & Team

If you have partners or a team, it is not unusual to find during the alignment process that the business units within your company contributing to projects and programs will not have consistent and appropriate start and completion times. For each major project or program, create an overall timeline to assure all of the sub-tasks are in alignment with the overall milestones. If project dates get changed... be sure to update the plans accordingly.

Create a Budget

Almost every activity in a business has a stream of revenue or expenses associated with it. Use your One Page Business Plan(s) to help identify all of the sources of revenue, expense and capital. If you need help in budgeting, get it. This is an important part of your success. Included in the Women in Business Tool Kit CD is a simple One Page Budget Worksheet that should be helpful.

Recommendation: If a practice, department, project, program or company is big enough for a One Page Business Plan, it should have a separate budget.

Implementation... Tracking & Measuring the Plan

Implement Your Plan

Many plans fail because they never get implemented! When great ideas sit on the shelf... nothing happens. Put your plan to work. You can bet your competitors are working on theirs!

Monitor & Measure

Create a Performance Scorecard for each Objective. Remember: Objectives, if well written, must have a numeric value that is graphable. Included in the Women in Business Tool Kit CD is a fun and easy template for creating Scorecards. You can graph your results against your Objectives, your Last Year Numbers and your Forecast Numbers (if appropriate)... you will have a visual picture of all the key metrics in your company. It is very simple and easy to determine if you are ahead of target... or behind.

Monthly Business Review

Recent surveys indicate only 1 in 5 businesses have a regularly scheduled monthly business review meeting to monitor the implementation and execution of their plans.

The monthly business review is a fabulous opportunity to learn what really happens in your business each month. Do a quick review of each of the major projects... are they on track? If not, address the issues and define solutions to get them back on track.

Have a business coach, professional advisor, mentor? Make it a practice to schedule an hour with them each month to review your progress against your plan.

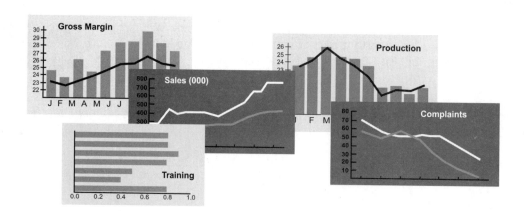

Filling in the Gaps

The process of writing a business plan, in some ways, is like writing a term paper on your business. You capture in writing what you know, conduct research to fill in the gaps, interview knowledgeable people, draft your document, ask for feedback, and then complete the final editing.

Your knowledge of your business is significant. Capture your initial thoughts in the first draft, and then begin the process of reflecting on your plan... and involving others. Keep in mind, the process of planning is one of continual reflection and refinement... and in many ways this is more important than the final document.

Most people have more resources instantly available to them than they realize. These people are very knowledgeable... and frequently free! They know you, your business, the industry, may share the same clients and may buy from the same vendors.

Over the years I have learned when I have a problem or run into a situation for the first time that is totally confusing and foreign to me the first place I turn is to my network of successful entrepreneurs, business owners and executives. They almost always have simple, practical solutions that work... and they offer them without expecting anything in return. Don't forget that your CPA, attorney, banker and vendors are excellent resources!

Other significant resources are the national associations (there are many that specifically exist to help women business owners) and online communities such as www.mominvented.com. Also, the Small Business Development Centers and microenterprise development organizations are great low cost (or no cost) sources of information and help. All of these organizations exist to follow the trends, innovations, opportunities, regulations, etc., we need to know about, and have access to, in order to be successful. Check out their websites... better yet, pick up the phone and talk with one of the executives. Get to know the regular contributors.

One of the benefits of The One Page Business Plan is that it can be read in less than five minutes. Share your plan with your resources. Invite their insights and feedback. Your plan will be stronger!

"Your Plan is not finished until it represents the best of your thinking!"

Sample Plans...

For some, the easiest way to learn how to write a plan is to take a look at how others have written their plans. In this section we have provided several sample plans for your review.

As you review these plans, you will note that they all follow the One Page Methodology fairly closely... but not necessarily... precisely. That's OK! Each of these plans is a real plan, written by an entrepreneur, business owner or executive. Their personal style comes through! It should... this is their business.

Note: Sample plans have these consistent characteristics

- Vision Statements paint a graphical picture of what is being built.
- Mission Statements are short, most are 8-12 words.
- Objectives are always graphable!
- Strategies describe how the company will be built.
- Action Plans describe the work to be done... all have completion dates.

Sample plans are real plans, but some of the authors requested their names, company names and locations be altered to protect their privacy.

"The One Page Plan methodology is extremely flexible.

Since 1994, over 500,000 One Page Plans have been created!"

Goldwaves Salon

Leslie Rice
Owner

vision

Within the next 3 years grow Goldwaves Salon into a $2,000,000 Fort Worth salon providing hair, skin and makeup products and services to women and men of all ages in the greater Dallas Fort Worth area.

mission

Creating Hair Love one strand at a time.

objectives

- Increase sales from $1.3M in 2009 to $1.45M in 2010.
- Increase retail sales from $306,000 to $372,000.
- Reduce costs of inventory from 55% to 50%.
- Increase gross margins from 40% to 47%.
- Reduce total payroll from 47% to 40%.
- Increase new clients from 1100 to 1700.
- Increase existing client retention from 81% to 90%.
- Increase new client retention rate from 43% to 57%.
- Increase pre-booking from 45% to 55%.

strategies

- Attract/solicit new clients by hiring a PR firm, networking groups., & corp. campaign.
- Tighten leadership accountability by utilizing One Page Plan, weekly mtgs, & set schedules.
- Improve clt. ret. w/ client rewards program, in-salon concierge, better software utilization.
- Improve pre-booking by 1:1, broadbands, client rewards, conversations in chair.
- Develop 12-week hiring process for styling, cut, color & personal education.
- Control expenses w/ rigid budget, enhanced communication by depts & eliminating waste.
- Improve retail w/ PR firm, create makeup experience, utilization of web.
- Improve payroll % by utilizing BBs, driving sales, hiring based on cash flow, huddles.

action plans

- Introduce PR firm by Jan 24.
- Build 12 week new hire system by March 27.
- Complete enhanced staff communication by March 31.
- Enhance social media program by Sept. 1.
- Complete new budget and accounting system by April 15.
- Develop client retention program by May 1.
- Initiate marketing research by July 7.
- Launch 2011 Action Plan by Nov. 1.
- Introduce makeup experience by Dec. 1.

California Knits

Mary Beth Miller
Entrepreneur, Founder, Machine Knitting Artist

vision

California Knits is a creative, soul-filled enterprise that provides:
• vibrant, unique, comfortable clothing as art for women.
• custom design capabilities for individual clients.
• training and mentoring of the next generation of machine knit artists.

Within 3 years California Knits will be a $5 million internationally recognized brand, serving the upscale fashion market for women who want to look and feel fabulous in knit clothing.

mission

Providing color, light, and energizing beauty in comfortable, natural fiber clothing.

objectives

• Achieve 2010 revenue of $1.5 million.
• Increase profit before tax from $110,000 to $175,000.
• Achieve profit margin of 50%.
• Hold production labor to 18% starting March 15th.
• Increase active store count to 20, an increase of 30% over FY2009.
• Outsource 50% of production by 4th quarter.
• Add 10 designs; 9 ready-to-wear; 1 gallery collectible. New sales $250,000.
• Attend at least 12 trade/trunk shows in 2010; book $750,000 in orders.

strategies

• Attract attention with stunning gallery quality garments priced at $2,000+.
• Design ready-to-wear products at affordable price points; $75 - $200.
• Outsource ready-to-wear; reserve personal time to create gallery garments.
• Develop professional team for production and operation of business.
• Cultivate relationships with upscale clients for referrals and shows.
• Explore avenues to entertainment industry for costume and personal clients.

action plans

• Develop budget and plans for capital needs for major expansion by 2/15.
• Contact six fashion magazines; present portfolio for publication on 4/20.
• Complete 8 ready-to-wear designs for show in Aspen in May.
• Attend national trunk shows: New York, Santa Fe and Carmel; Q2 + Q3.
• Purchase and install 3 new computer aided knitted machines by 6/30.
• Complete redesign of display booths for winter fairs by 10/31.
• Complete installation of CRM system by 10/31. New GL by 12/31.

Shea Therapeutic Equestrian Center

Dana Butler-Moburg
Executive Director

vision

With the next three years, grow the Shea Center into a preeminent $2 million organization providing therapeutic equestrian activities to a diverse community of people with special needs, and providing internationally recognized education to therapeutic equestrian professionals.

mission

Improve the lives of people with disabilities through therapeutic horse-related programs.

objectives

- Expand operating campaign to $1.7 Million.
- Raise $1.5 Million through capital campaign.
- Increase annual fund to $250,000.
- Implement bilingual programming with 12 families.
- Increase community awareness by 50%.
- Raise $500,000 by June 30 through Campaign Committee leadership.

strategies

- Core services include therapeutic riding, hippotherapy, and non-mounted activities.
- Raise capital funds using new campaign committee.
- Redesign and staff annual fund and face-face giving program.
- Increase public awareness through community speaking and media relations.
- Develop campaign prospects through new Board connections.
- Maintain development focus thru weekly review mtgs.
- Develop more effective budget, cost control, reporting systems.
- Dana to be more involved in developing prospects, solicitation and stewardship.

action plans

- Implement budget & cost control program (1/15).
- Hire new business manager to take on operational responsibilities (3/15).
- Recreate Campaign Committee by (4/30).
- Develop community speaking program (6/30). Deliver monthly talks in Fall.
- Staff Board, all Committees (6/30). Board Training (Sept)
- Launch monthly development meetings (6/15); biweekly (9/15).
- Complete equestrian facility (7/31), offices (11/30).
- Recruit 5 Comm members (8/31), ID prospect list (9/30), develop new materials (9/30)

Pam Hutchinson, Realtor

Pam Hutchinson
Owner

vision

Within the next 2 years grow Pam Hutchinson, Realtor into a $ 20,000 comprehensive, customer-oriented real estate business in the Middle Tennessee area providing exceptional customer service, including access to multiple MLS search capabilities, to individuals and families either buying or selling commercial or residential property in Dover, TN and surrounding areas.

mission

Moving up or just moving on... everyone's a winner

objectives

- Increase revenue from $1,600 to $20,000.
- Raise pre-tax profits from a loss of $6,300 to a profit of $15,000.
- Decrease annual percentage of unsold listed properties from 50% to 33%.
- Boost average annual listings from 6 to 12; one per month.
- Increase average monthly growth of prospect list from 1 to 3.
- Increase annual trips to visit family/friends from 2 to 3.
- Reduce # of training hours from 100 to 20.
- Decrease avg work week from 7 days to 3 days.

strategies

- Assure excel cust svc w/ timely follow-up, excpt prod knowl base and lots of hustle.
- Use Internet/Tech to communicate with clients, maintain records and mkt business.
- Mkt bus by local networking, local advertising and high qual print & electr materials
- Focus business with OPBP, on-going bus coaching and giving up second job.
- Build aware of local prop w/ rev of daily updates, reg prop previews and pers contact.
- Prom prof growth w/ cont CEU's, reading prof journals, internet rsrch & peer trng.
- Prov self care w/ trips to see fam/friends, no 2nd job, & more qual time w/spouse.
- Assure profit by incr prspt client base, reduc expen and creating passive inc sources
- Control expenses by reduc trng, reduc/reuse/recycle, smart choices & peer bulk prch.

action plans

- Implement Updated Marketing Plan by March 15.
- Launch Knowledge Base Improvement Program by March 31.
- Hire Business Coach by May 1.
- Build at least one source of Passive Income by June 1.
- Launch Family and Friends Travel Plan by June 30.
- Complete Technology Update by July 1.
- Launch new Web Site by August 1.
- Complete first phase of Biz Focus Project by October 1.
- Complete Limited Annual Training Plan by November 30.

Esteem Music Academy

Mary Walby
Founder, Senior Piano Instructor

vision

Within the next year grow Esteem Music Academy into an in-demand Western Whatcom County piano school providing private and group piano instruction, from novice to intermediate level, performance, technique, and theory education, concerts, and team and life building skills, ages 7 to 10, accompany church services, receptions and weddings with $75K sales.

mission

Experiencing fun playing music and building confidence.

objectives

- Achieve sales of 75K in 2010.
- Hire 4 p/t employees/consultants by Jan 15th.
- Add 17 new clients; 7 by Feb 15th, 10 by May 15th.
- Increase number of concerts from 1 to 2 per month by April 1st.
- Increase from 1 to 2 number of music teachers by June 1st.
- Develop a Strategic Alliance Program with 8 members by Aug 15th.
- Increase hourly rate to $60 by Sept 30th.
- Create Esteem Music Method by Oct 1st.

strategies

- Focus on children ages 7-10 and beginners.
- Become regionally known as a music school that provides life skills.
- Focus on training grammar schools in affluent neighborhoods.
- Core products/services are 1:1 music classes, group sessions, and accompaniments.
- Promote initial trial of Practice Cards for students AND Esteem Cards for their parents.
- Pricing strategy is value-based, develop marketing funnel and increase rates.
- Hire bookkeeper, music teacher, administrative person, and house cleaner.
- Use technology to market online, automate/streamline systems, develop future curriculum.
- Create processes for hiring, operations manual, and framework for curriculum.

action plans

- Develop Pricing Structure (Jan).
- Create client intake process (Jan).
- Build blog or Wiki for curriculum development (Mar).
- Schedule 4 speaking events and 2 concerts (Mar).
- Develop company brand by June 1st.
- Hire 4 employees/consultants by Aug 15th.
- Expand internet presence w/shopping cart by Oct 15th.
- Develop 2 products by Nov 15th.
- Create operations manual by Dec 31st.

Christina Ecklund Design

Christina Ecklund
Owner

vision

Within the next 3-5 years grow Christina Ecklund Design into a $500,000 national fashion jewelry business providing unique trend and classic jewelry and fashion accessories to women ages 24 - 50, who want to be unique but not spend a fortune ($60 - $145). Each piece is designed and handcrafted in the USA.

mission

Create stunning jewelry and accessories that are as unique and special as the women who wear them.

objectives

- Achieve 2010 sales of $24,000.
- Earn pre-tax profits of $12,000.
- Add 20 new accounts; 10 in 1st half, 10 in 2nd half.
- Increase average sale from $60 to $400. Encourage multiples in ordering.
- Increase repeat purchase rate from 50% to 95%.
- Send out product samples to stores and contact for feed back or order.
- Sell 200 units of jewelry at average price of $120.
- Deliver 100% of orders (all made to order in the 1st & 2nd quarter) on time.

strategies

- Focus on wholesale & retail markets. Find retailers specifically geared to my target.
- Attract/solicit new wholesale buyers & retail customers.
- Focus on trade show, direct store marketing & fashion trends. Get my name out there.
- Core Product is unique well priced designer jewelry and accessories.
- Our pricing strategy is keep prices in the mid range, focus on multiple sales.
- Encourage repeat purchases by offering new products on a regular basis.
- Create website where people can shop my products as well as link to stores.
- Increase awareness in the market with periodicals, working with buyers & trade shows.
- Grow business at 10% per year by adding new products, new divisions & promotions.

action plans

- Hire a small work force to fabricate my designs and fill orders by Jan 15th.
- Create internal shipping department by April 15th.
- Show line at Los Angeles gift show in Sept.
- Create web site with shopping capabilities to increase revenue by Aug 15th.
- Display at Las Vegas Fashion Magic show Oct 5-7.
- Introduce Fancy Bird Studio (Teen Line) by Oct 1st.
- Hire and streamline work force using outside labor sources by Nov 15th.
- Design and fabricate Spring Line to present at Gift Show San Francisco in Aug.

Eti-Kits
Sharyn Amoroso
Owner

vision

Within the next 3 years grow Eti-Kits into a $1 million company through sales of booklets, DVD's, and accessories. Establish brand recognition so that "Eti-Kits" becomes synonymous with the essential tools and guides needed to learn good manners in today's world, while positioning myself as the new spokesperson for etiquette.

mission

Bring the ease of learning good manners to anyone.
Simplifying what people need to know to be their best!

objectives

- Achieve 2010 gross sales of $90,000 in customized booklets.
- Increase internet sales of products to $10,000.
- Reduce credit line balance and loans to less than $10,000 by year end.
- Add 15 corporate accounts for bulk orders of booklets generating $6,000 each by Jan 30th.
- Sell Eti-Kits line of products to major corporation for $5 million within 5 years.
- Generate $5,000/month in speaker fees starting June 30th.

strategies

- Core products are etiquette mini-guides, DVD's, Napkin Clips, accessories.
- National pitch with different angles for various markets timed with seasonal issues.
- Target broad base of clients to determine where interest and sales translate best.
- Methodically grow "Eti-Kits" name recognition by PR printed media, TV, internet.
- Raise my nat'l profile as leading etiquette spokesperson via news, mags, TV, internet.
- Focus on parenting, higher education, and business professional markets.
- Pursue HR Depts of major corporations for sales of mini-guides for employees.
- Continue personal education in the field of social, business, and military etiquette.

action plans

- Hire intern to sell mini-guides to HR Depts. w/1,000 employees by 1/15.
- Hire PR to launch blitz of Napkin Clips to parenting & family markets by 2/15.
- Expand internet exposure and sales via Amazon, Facebook, LinkedIn, PSOW by 3/15.
- PR to blitz Napkin Clips to food & travel, senior & special needs markets by 6/1.
- Complete first draft of Children's mini-guide by 8/15.
- Plan production of Dining DVD with videographer by 9/15.
- PR to establish Sharyn as expert spokesperson to TV & print media by year end.

Fresno Film Studio

Gladys Deniz
Executive Director

vision

Within the next 3 years build a non-profit sound stage film studio and screen play/stage theater for local high school students in Fresno county with an annual funding goal of $150,000.

mission

We help high school students share their life story on film.

objectives

- Raise initial $250,000 capital to build a sound stage film studio by Jan 31st.
- Generate $150,000 on-going operating budget for student film productions annually.
- Recruit 100 liberal arts students into 4-year film study program by March 31st.
- Achieve 100% participation of film students in annual Slick Rock film festival.
- Place 70% of students into summer film workshops at SF Academy of Arts.
- Evaluate program goals with student pre-eval (Sept) and post-eval (June) annually.

strategies

- Hold informational film study program meetings with local 8th grade students.
- Increase awareness of student films with production screenings at local theaters.
- Focus on YouTube & Internet trends for student film distribution opportunities.
- Hold fundraisers at local film theaters selling 250 Wall of Fame bricks for $100 ea.
- Focus on 15 high-end local film producers to rent studio 10 days/yr @ $1,000/day.
- Invest in HD & 3D technology to attract local film producer investors.
- Research state and federal grant funding opportunities & solicit donor support.

action plans

- Partner w/Washington High School to add film production to their academy by Jan 15th.
- Hire project manager to secure grant funding and construction proposals by 3/15.
- Visit bay area high schools with film production studios for construction ideas by 4/30.
- Consult w/ Stephen Burum regarding equipping student sound stages, July.
- Announce studio project at fall conference of Fresno Filmmakers Alliance, Oct.
- Complete design plan for studio construction by 12/31.

Z-TEC, Inc. – Consolidated Plan

Cynthia Johnson
CEO

vision

Within the next three years build Z-TEC, Inc. into a $2 billion global provider of integrated workflow management solutions for Fortune 1000 companies, major municipalities and significant governmental agencies at the country, state, regional and federal level. Z-TEC, Inc. will be headquartered in San Francisco with offices in New York, Dallas, London, Singapore and Rio de Janeiro.

mission

Building Industrial Strength Business Systems!

Our systems improve productivity, and reduce the costs of maintenance, materials, and facilities for large process oriented companies and municipalities.

objectives

• Achieve 2010 Revenue of at least $900 Million.
• Increase Profit before Interest & Taxes from $60 to $85 Million.
• Complete at least 300 new installations and obtain 500 new clients.
• Migrate at least 250 existing clients to Z-TEC web product cost reduction program.
• Increase Gross Margin from 51% to 55% through product cost reduction program.
• Increase sales per field employee from $250,000 to $300,000 by 9/30.
• Reduce Accounts Receivables from 60 days to 45 days.
• Achieve FTE head count of 1,500 by 11/30.

strategies

• Growth: Grow 50% each year by development of new clients and migration of existing clients.
• Reputation: Product position & strong reputation from existing client/partner referrals.
• Partnering: Align with industry leaders, partnering for marketing & solution development.
• Competitive Position: Optimize user/based pricing & modular system concepts for flexibility.
• Product Approach: Configure rather than Customize, Business Rules vs. custom programs.
• R&D: WorkFlow Solutions, Open Systems, multiple environments, Object-Oriented, flexible.
• Develop aligned team, know the plan, have sense of urgency, responsibility & accountability.
• Develop Employee Incentive Program to allow the team to share in the rewards & have fun.

action plans

• Implement Power Partner Initiatives w/Oracle UK by 3/31.
• Complete development of the Z-TEC client/server product by 3/31.
• Develop Sales & Marketing Resource Plan by 4/31.
• Develop Partner strategies w/PeopleSoft, Sun Micro, IBM by 4/30.
• Launch Europe Customer Forum in London at June 08 Convention.
• Develop Sales Force Automation Plan by August, implement in 4th Quarter.
• Implement financial reporting system at project/dept. level by Oct. 31.
• Implement professional skills development program by Nov. 30.

Z-TEC Inc. – Southern European Sales Division

Alexis Morgan
Sales Division Mgr.

vision

Within the next three years grow the southern Europe division of Z-TEC into a $150 million business unit with offices in Madrid, Barcelona, Nice and Florence.

mission

Find customers… close contracts!

objectives

- Increase sales from $35 to $45 million.
- Complete installation of 50 systems.
- Increase gross margins from 51 to 55% by increasing sale of value added services.
- Increase contribution margin to $20 million.
- Migrate at least 35 existing clients to Z-TEC internet product by 12/31.
- Reduce accounts receivable from 60 to 45 days.
- Achieve FTE head count of 275 by 9/31.

strategies

- Partners: Align with industry leaders, partnering for marketing & solution development.
- Product Approach: Configure rather than customize business rules vs. custom programs.
- Market Positioning; modular systems for flexibility, customization; premium pricing.
- R&D: Workflow solutions, open systems, multi-platform, object-oriented, flexible.
- Develop an aligned team with sense of urgency, responsibility and accountability.
- Develop employee incentive programs to allow the team to share rewards.

action plans

- Implement Power Partner Initiatives w/Oracle Spain by 5/31.
- Launch European Customer Forum in Spain at June convention.
- Develop Sales Force Automation Plan by 08/31, implement in 4th quarter.
- Implement financial reporting system at project/dept level by 10/31.
- Implement professional skills development program by 11/15.
- Complete Portugal facilities upgrades by 12/15.
- Complete communication & team performance training w/12 branch mgrs. by 3/31.

Lessons Learned from Consultants...

Since 2002, I've worked with hundreds of women to get their very best thinking about what they're building – on a single page. I've seen women go from overwhelmed or confused -- to clear, focused and ready to make it happen! The very act of clearly stating what they are building, honing in on their critical numbers, creating clear strategies for each of them and outlining the projects that will make them a reality is empowering and calming. One of my clients says this: "Your plan needs to be in writing. It's easy -- with help. It will get you thinking clearly!"

Toni Nell
Springboard Consulting
www.springboardconsulting.biz

Listen to the part of you that knows what's right for you. Let your direction for your business come from within, rather than letting outside influences dictate your direction. Creating your One Page Plan will give your "super-sized" vision and mission form and structure. It will serve as a lighthouse helping you keep the faith, reminding you where you are headed and what is truly yours to do—and what is not!

Linda Anderson, MBA
Prosperity Circles
www.prosperitycircles.com

I refer my clients to the OPBP so that they can quickly (and easily) create a level of clarity for the intention of their goals. The OPBP process helps business leaders and entrepreneurs identify their vision, mission and strategies in a manner to access the richness of their intuitive brilliance. In my experience, that is the key that helps people align who they are with what they do (or create) – the formula for creating thriving success.

Dory Willer, SPHR, PCC, 2003 International Coach of the Year
Beacon Quest Coaching
www.BeaconQuest.com

Thirty years ago I went from a clerk to a Wall Street Trader in three years. I had very specific goals and worked my plan consistently. Today as an advisor to entrepreneurs and small business owners my best advice is to 1) develop a specific niche, 2) get other people to market for you, by marketing for them, 3) have a One Page Plan and work it religiously and 4) no matter what anyone else says -- never, ever, give up on your goals!

Maria Marsala
Elevating Your Business
www.elevatingyourbusiness.com

Some women in business, especially those who provide expertise, spend a great deal of time, energy and worry about whether they are providing enough value to justify their fees. I have also found that men rarely have the same level of concern. Many of the notions we have that hold us back, lie just outside of our awareness. Your One Page Plan is a process and discipline for thinking through the value you bring to your customers and clarifies the best ways to make what you have to offer available to your customers.

Nora Wolfson
N.E.W. Associates
www.norawolfsonconsulting.com

As a woman in business it is critical to be brave and disciplined. I've learned as a business owner consultant that if you're not brave enough to expose your brilliant and not-so-brilliant ideas, get back up when you fall down, act transparently inside and outside of the workplace, disciplined enough to regularly revisit strategy, and stick to the sound execution of your plan, it will be difficult to be successful overtime. I have a One Page Plan for my business; it's how I stay disciplined.

Shannon Ryan
Spectra Learning Group
www.spectralearning.com

that Help Women Write One Page Business Plans

We see that one of the key success indicators is a well honed, concisely crafted and communicated business plan. Women often come to business leadership feeling as if they have to 'do it all themselves'. For the last five years we have used The One Page Business Plan as a facilitated process, often in groups of 5 -10. This offers a platform for stimulated thinking and collaborative writing. What emerges are inspired and articulate plans the outcome of which is the ability to lead businesses, from solopreneurships to large organizations, in the living of their visions, intentions and commitments to action.

Brenda Chaddock & Carollyne Conlinn
Limitless Leadership Inc.
www.limitlessleadership.com

Having started and successfully exited several businesses, one learning curve I faced over and over again was my determination to go it alone. Fortunately, when I began building the business that grew into a multimillion dollar company, I had learned to get help! We tend to resist getting help because we think we know everything, don't want to spend the money and really don't have the time. Even though I am stellar at helping others, I work with a consultant to keep me on track. Getting outside input is vital. I have a One Page Plan; so do all of my clients. It is simple, and it works!

Cynthia Riggs
Women Building Business
www.womenbuildingbusiness.com

Everything needs a blueprint! The One Page Business Plan is the easiest way to blueprint a business, profit center, department, project or program. The simplicity of the process energizes people. It helps them articulate their goals, desires, plans. The One Page Business Plan is a tool they can work with and understand. I use it with all of my clients.

Pat Poyle (former Advertising Director, Saturn Division, General Motors)
President, Henry Business Solutions
www.henrysolutions.net

When women want to start a business venture, whether it's a profit or nonprofit, it's usually because they believe their venture can make a difference. But women still are uniquely challenged with the demands of work and caring for others so it's essential to make space for the energy required to get the venture started. The One Page Business Plan is a powerful process that gives life and structure to the business idea and creates that space to work in. It's hard not to be impressed with a finely crafted One Page Business Plan. In fact, it is so much easier for a woman entrepreneur to get the respect, support and even backing she needs to start that venture when she has a plan on paper.

Catherine Marshall
Capbuilders
www.capbuilders.org

Acknowledgements

This book could not have been created without the incredible work of hundreds of our dedicated One Page consultants who have helped thousands of women entrepreneurs craft their One Page Business Plans over the last ten years. To them we express a deep heart-felt thanks!

To list all of the people who contributed in little and big ways to make this book possible would take multiple pages. However we would like to express our gratitude to all of the women who were willing to share their entire One Page Business Plans so that other women could learn from them.

We would also like to thank the dozens of women who shared their stories about their businesses and how they have used their One Page Business Plans to launch and build successful businesses.

A special thanks goes to the women who shared their poignant sage advice... these are true treasures to be re-read and reflected on multiple times.

A final thank you goes to the fifteen women who went through an intensive One Page Business Plan book camp earlier this year to produce a set of diverse and truly unique One Page Business Plans.

Nuge Ajouz

Sharyn Amoroso

PJ Anderson

Linda Anderson

Heather Bailey

Chanda Beck

Wendy Beckerman

Diane Beckman

Cathy Bennett

Allison Bliss

Pat Brown

Dana Butler-Moburg

Brenda Chaddock

Lyn Ciocca

Maxine Clark

Carollyne Conlinn

Gail Patton DaMert

Gladys Deniz

Diane Dixon

Tonya Dorsey

Dana Dworin

Christina Ecklund

Amy Faust

Nina Feldman

Gwen Gallagher

Lara Galloway

Clarine Hardesty

Leslie Haywood

Sue Holmes

Tracy Holzman

Karen Horrigan

Pam Hutchinson

Kathleen Ion

Diane Jarmolow

Deborah Johnson

Mindy Jones

Christy Mariani

Catherine Marsh

Maria Marsala

Catherine Marshall

Gwen Martin

Pat Mathews

Toni Nell

Greta Olano

Sarah Oliver

Pam Pillers

Christin Powell

Pat Poyle

Nika Quirk

Cheryl Rebottaro

Cheryl Ries

Cynthia Riggs

Cindy Rossman

Diane Ruebling

Shannon Ryan

Jessica Siegel

Rebecca Solome Shaw

April Sheldon

Jan St. John

Luanne Stevenson

Nicola Ries Taggart

Tracy Tamura

Christine Tande

Kathy Tierney

Tina Traum

Mary Walby

Elisabeth Watson

Dory Willer

Nora Wolfson

Marian Woodard

Cynthia Wrasman

Patrice Wynne

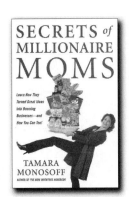

The One Page Business Plan...
Now a Best-Selling Series!

For the Creative Entrepreneur

This is the million-dollar best seller that forever changed the way people write business plans. This is the fastest, easiest way for creative entreprenuers and small business owners to write a business plan!

For the Professional Consultant

New to consulting? Need to move your practice to the next level? This book was written by consultants, for consultants. It contains everything you need to create a blueprint for a successful consulting practice... all on a single page.

For Non-Profit Organizations

If you are responsible for starting, managing or funding a non-profit... this book was written for you. One Page Plans create a community culture of discipline and accountability. This process helps executives, employees, volunteers and boards clearly define and live up to their promises.

For Financial Services Professionals

Industry leaders in insurance, banking and financial services demanded we create this special edition for their industry. If you make your living selling financial products or services or managing people that do... this book was written for you!

For the Creative Entrepreneur (Spanish Edition)

This is the Spanish language version of the million-dollar best seller that forever changed the way people write and implement business plans.

For Women in Business

Finally, a business planning book for women in business! It combines Jim Horan's proven methodology with Tamara Monosoff's experience, insights, colorful stories and real business plans from women all over the country.

Available at www.onepagebusinessplan.com/books

(For quantity pricing call: 510-705-8400)

And local bookstores, Amazon & other online retailers!

Need More? We Can Help!

Executives with Management or Sales Teams

Over the last nineteen years we have helped hundreds of executive teams implement The One Page Business Plan® Process... usually in less than four weeks! Each executive, business unit manager and project team creates their One Page Plan which is in alignment with the overall company's plan. You can then monitor results monthly with our web-based Planning and Performance System with online Scorecards and Progress Reports. Interested? Visit us on the web for a short video about this system.

Business Owners

There is a new breed of woman business owner in the marketplace today. They are either starting up new businesses or reinventing established ones. They are intensely passionate, competitive and dedicated. They care about people, the environment, and their communities. They don't run their businesses casually. If you are one of those women, you'll appreciate the focus, discipline and results you'll achieve by implementing One Page Plans in your business. Call now or visit us on the web.

Entrepreneurs, Small Business and Startups

Today's small business issues are complex, resources are limited, and time is of the essence. There's no room for mistakes. You have to think fast and move faster. What this requires is an innovative, fresh approach to business planning... one designed to act as a catalyst for your ideas. The One Page Business Plan is a powerful tool for building and managing your business. It's short, concise, and it delivers your plan quickly and effectively. There can be no question as to where you are going when it's in writing!

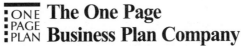

ONE PAGE PLAN **The One Page Business Plan Company**

Consulting • Training • Web Based Performance Management Systems

510.705.8400 • www.onepagebusinessplan.com/women

Women in Business Tool Kit
How to Install and Use the CD

Installation Instructions:

Simply load the CD into your CD drive. requires Microsoft
Word® and/or Excel® to use the templates, forms and
spreadsheets. Open any Directory with a double-click.
Select desired Word® document or Excel® spreadsheet.

CAUTION:

Immediately after opening any of the files we encourage you to save
the file with a new name using the "SAVE AS" command in order
to preserve the original content of the file.

No Technical Support

This CD is provided without technical or software support. Please
refer to your Microsoft Word® or Excel® User Manuals for questions
related to the use of these software programs.

System Requirements:

Windows 95/98/NT/2000/XP/Vista
Macintosh OS 9.1 or higher
Microsoft Word® and Excel®
CD/ROM drive